Divination by Runes
Using The Haindl Rune Oracle Cards

By

Nigel Pennick

U.S. GAMES
SYSTEMS, INC

U.S. GAMES SYSTEMS, INC.
Publishers
Stamford, CT 06902 USA

First edition

Library of Congress Cataloging-in-Publication Data

Pennick, Nigel.
  The Haindl Rune Oracle: Divination by Runes Using Haindl Rune
  Oracle Cards/by Nigel Pennick.
       p.   cm.
  Includes bibliographical references.
  ISBN 1-57281-025-4
  1. Fortune-telling by runes. 2. Tarot cards. 3. Haindl, Herman.
       4. Runes-Miscellanea.   I. Title
BF1779.R86P45 1997
133.3'3--DC21   97-41146
                                                   CIP

                  99   10 9 8 7 6 5 4 3 2 1

                       Printed in Canada

                  U.S. GAMES SYSTEMS, INC.
                    Stamford, CT 06902 USA

CONTENTS

FOREWORD

This work is concerned with the runes, those mystic characters of an "alphabet" whose history stretches back into times quite different from the present—some 2,200 years ago. From their inception, recorded in sacred myth, the runes have been special, rarely used casually. In former times, those possessing a knowledge of the runes and everything that goes with them—the rune-masters—were the wise women and men of their times. As the runes were handed down from generation to generation, often under harsh and secret circumstances, a body of lore accumulated, which was added to by each fresh generation of rune-masters. This process has led to the knowledge and lore that we possess today, when the runes have outgrown their original socio-cultural milieu and have become an established part of "world culture."

Unlike many esoteric and magical traditions, the runes are not and have never been controlled by a centralized authority: there is no priesthood of runecraft. This makes rune studies a very open area. There is a body of generally accepted authentic lore, and also a considerable body of myth and speculation. These are contained in a number of books and in the systems of rune-practice derived from them. Today, in many parts of the world, there are practitioners of runic divination, runic astrology, runic numerology, runic cryptography, runic meditation, runic exercise, rune-magic, and runic art. This healthy diversity attests to the continuing vitality of the runes, over 2,000 years after their inception.

Although the runes are one of Europe's most ancient oracles, this does not mean that they cannot be used in a modern way and remain true to themselves. Only fundamentalists express the impossible wish to return to the past, to ignore the history which has come between then and now. The present, including this book, is an expression of the sum total of all things which have happened to date. So it is impossible to undertake a return to past conditions. We must go forward, using the best of the old and the best of the new, a principle known in the United States as *retronuevo*, upon which this study is founded. Today's greater human awareness of our place as one of the earth's life-forms is a reclaiming of the once-discarded wisdom of ancient times. The ancient, intuitive view of the world order can take its rightful place again alongside the intellectual, rational discoveries of science. In this way, the regeneration of the spiritual life of the earth can accompany the restoration of a sane approach to the physical environment of this planet.

The runes are far more than just the archaic characters of an ancient, disused alphabet—they are true symbols. Symbols are a means of accessing the inward workings of the human mind. They are like doors to the subconscious, and this is a description which has been given to the runes. Of course, like any living system, the runes have grown and altered over the years, and, as a vital current, are still undergoing change and development. This present work is an example of this organic process. Although these venerable characters are part of an ancient and powerful oracle, they are manifested here in a completely modern way through the media of the printed word and printed cards, which themselves are reproductions of paintings by Hermann Haindl. His paintings are unique insights into the deeper meanings of the runes, extending the boundaries of perception into hitherto-untapped realms. This book, too, covers previously unexplored areas of divination using runes, complementing the cards' fresh insights.

In the past, the runes have suffered a perverted use at the hands of unscrupulous politicians. In the earlier part of this century, political extremists discovered their value as ready-made magically emotive symbols for the adornment of the uniforms and banners of their militaristic organizations. Fortunately, this time is past. The misusers of the runic power paid dearly for their sacrilege. The disrespectful misuse of an ancient symbol does not pervert its inner meaning, and here in this work, the archaic and eternal meanings of the runes reign supreme, untouched by the distorting influence of totalitarian creeds. Northern Tradition spirituality, of which the runes are an important part, stands for the freedom of the individual, and that individual's personal spiritual progress according to his or her own destiny.

The rune oracle is grounded in the common spiritual tradition of Europe north of the Alps, which has an origin in the shamanry of the last Ice Age 12,000 years ago, if not much earlier in the dim archaic past before the ice came. While it deals with the many aspects of the runes, this book is concerned mainly with the runes as an oracle, using the Haindl Rune Oracle Cards. Previous rune card decks, of which there have been only a handful, have either just borne the runic characters, or have used tarot-like imagery. These cards are a unique departure from this approach. The images, based on the forms of the runes, have many layers of meaning, like the runes themselves. They represent the various appropriate aspects of the primal forces that underlie the runes, and, indeed, all human experience.

To begin work with the runes and to use them as a means to self-awareness, one should learn their form and meanings. These cards and this book are the means to that end. Equally, in a divination, the way in which the runic cards fall can give an experienced rune-user a great deal of information. One's question may only be a beginning: the runes may well reveal information and insights which the questor did not suspect. Often, the runes can reveal to the inquirer unconscious information which may come as a great surprise. That is their primary function. But, as with the other great esoteric systems of the world, the most profound wisdom of the runes cannot be expressed in words at all. Hermann Haindl's paintings for the cards are a pictorial vision of those runic qualities which are only partially expressible in words. They show us that, at the most fundamental level, the runes serve as a mirror of our own level of spiritual development, and our own state of harmony with other human beings and the world in general.

PART 1
THE RUNES: THEIR ORIGIN, HISTORY, AND MEANING

"Because there are innumerable things beyond the range of human understanding, we constantly use symbolic terms to represent concepts that we cannot fully comprehend."

— C.G. Jung

ORIGINS AND MEANING

The written character known as a rune is thought of primarily as a character in an ancient, and to most people, strange alphabet called the *Futhark*. But this is far from the whole matter, for a rune is primarily an arcanum whose outward expression is only the visible character or stave. A rune is a profound secret concept, which cannot be explained completely in words, but only grasped intuitively. Part of the mystery of the runes is their origin, which is recorded only in mythological terms. There is no historical record of their genesis, only enigmatic, sometimes contradictory, archaeological remains from the earliest times when runes may have come into being. However, many researchers have attempted to unravel this historical mystery. These endeavors have led to a number of mutually-exclusive theories.

During the 1870s, a Danish investigator, L. F. A. Wimmer, suggested that runes were merely altered versions of the Roman alphabet, created by a single individual to serve as a cryptic code. His theory was elaborated by Sigurd Agrell, who claimed, not very convincingly, that the runes were derived from a cursive Latin script. Others thought differently. In 1904, D. von Friesen contended that runes were derived from the Greek alphabet, and used first by the Goths. The most plausible theory, backed up by archaeological remains, was put forward by C. J. S. Marstrander and M. Hammarström, in 1928 and 1930 respectively. This theory contends that the runes were derived from the North Italic (Etruscan) alphabet. A "hoard" of 26 bronze helmets discovered in 1812 at Negau (now near the border between Austria and Slovenia) is almost conclusive evidence for this theory. One of these bears a Germanic votive inscription in North Italic characters, written from right to left. Transliterated, the inscription reads *harigasti teiva*, "to the god, Harigast" (possibly a deity of warriors). Many of the North Italic letters look very "runic," and it is probable that this alphabet was taken and modified into a magical tool by an individual magus somewhere in the Alps around the year 200 B.C. Staves with North Italic characters inscribed on them, which can only have served as divinatory wands, have been discovered at Kitzbühel in the Tyrol. This area is likely to be close to the birthplace of the runes.

Reasonable suggestions that runes were derived ultimately from another, earlier, alphabet, were rejected violently by racist "historians" of the Nazi period. In keeping with their xenophobic beliefs, they insisted that the runes were exclusively "Nordic Aryan" in origin, and, on the contrary, were the base from which the Roman and Greek alphabets were derived. Of course, this contention is completely untenable, being nothing more than crude propaganda designed to further political ambitions.

That the Futhark was an individual creation is clear both from archaeological and epigraphic studies, and from ancient tradition. It is probable that certain symbols, such as those still extant on rock surfaces near Golling in Austria, at Val Camonica in Italy, and at several other locations in the Alps, were used for divination before the discovery of the runic Futhark. But the runic Futhark as we know it came into being when some of these earlier signs became identified with and augmented by certain characters from an transalpine alphabet, creating a uniquely flexible system of writing and symbolism. That was a rare moment in history when both the analytical and the intuitive sides of the brain were unified in response to a single symbol. This act of creative insight is told of in the legend of the discovery of the runes by Odin, where what appears to be a shamanic ritual is described. In ancient Norse scripture we can read:

—⟋⟍—

I know that I hung on the wind-blown tree,

Through nine days and nine nights,

I was stabbed with a spear, and sacrificed to Odin,

Me, given to myself, on that tree,

Which no man knows from which roots it rises,

They helped me neither with bread,

Nor with drinking horn,

I took the runes.

Screaming, I took them,

Then I fell back from that place.

(Hávamál, stanzas 138 and 139)

—⟋⟍—

The shamanic experience described in this poem appears to involve the speaker being crucified on a sacred tree for the magical period of nine days and nights. This experience seems to have generated a tormented flash of insight which allowed the shaman, who is named as Odin, to realize the full potential of the runes for human use. It is notable that Odin does not create the runes from out of nowhere, but wrests them from the universal source and renders them available for use by others.

The runic system is a powerful spiritual tool because, unlike the letters of the Roman alphabet, which are strictly utilitarian, every rune has its own meaningful name with corresponding symbolic and magical connections. Some of the names describe a physical object, such as a yew tree or the sun, while others refer to qualities or experiences like joy and possession. The actual name of the rune is not the end of the matter, however. Each name refers to a whole complex system of concepts and correspondences. By using individual runes, or combinations of runes, there is no aspect of human experience that cannot be investigated or described in detail, as this book and its accompanying card deck demonstrate.

We can only understand the runes fully in terms of the world-view of the Northern Tradition. (The Northern Tradition is that religious and cultural system which contains the common elements of Germanic, Norse, and Celtic beliefs, dating from pre-Christian times and continued in folk stories and customs to this day.) The beliefs, legends, traditions, and way of life of this vanished age are preserved and encapsulated within the meanings ascribed to the runes. Fortunately, these ancient meanings were preserved in three Rune Poems: the Old English, the Norwegian, and the Icelandic. The Old English poem is believed to date from the eleventh century, but with elements which date from the eighth century. In its present form, the Norwegian poem comes from the thirteenth century, while the Icelandic is of the fifteenth century. It is clear that all of these manuscript poems are copies of earlier editions, and their close correspondences in runic description suggest that they may be derived from a common ancestral rune poem, now lost.

A study of the rune-meanings in the rune poems shows that runes have always had a magical as well as a utilitarian use. They have served for magic, ritual, and divination as well as an alternative form of writing to the Roman alphabet. The Common Germanic Futhark, sometimes misleadingly called The Longer Rune-Row, and more commonly known as The Elder Futhark, contains 24 runic characters in a specific order. It is known as a "Futhark" and not as an "alphabet" because the first six runes in the sequence are F, U, Th, A, R, K.

Linguistically, the word "rune" has connotations of mystery. The word is believed to come originally from the Indo-European root *ru,* which meant "a mysterious or secret thing." In the early Anglo-Saxon poem, *Beowulf,* the king's counselor is called a *Runwita,* "a wise man knowing secrets." The Old German word *runa,* which meant "a whisperer," is believed to have referred to "one who knows," a wise woman or man. Likewise, the Old Norse word *run* means "a secret or mystery." In Middle Welsh, the same meaning is borne by *rhin,* and in Old Irish, *run.* In the Scottish dialect of English, the word *roun* means "to whisper" or "to speak much and often about one thing." In German, the word *raunen* also has connections to secrecy and mystery.

But what is the "mystery" of the runes? The idea of "mystery" inherent in the runes could have come from the secret of letters in an age of illiteracy, except for the recurrent connection of runes with magic. For example, in Britain, the rown-tree or rowan tree is a tree associated with magical protection. Its red berries are known in Scotland as *rowns,* and the old Scottish adage "rowan tree and red threid gar the witches tyne their speed" ("rowan tree and red thread make the witches lose their speed") emphasizes the magic power of the runes as expressed through the sacred tree. More specifically, this refers to binding magic, as evidenced by the red thread.

Tree-lore is an important part of alphabetic studies in the Northern Tradition, for it is related directly to a number of runic characters. Various trees correspond directly with all of the letters of the Ogham tree-alphabet that was restricted to Britain and Ireland, and thus used less widely than the runes. Unfortunately, few writers seem to have given alphabetic tree-lore the importance it deserves. The form of divination known as the Oracle of the Fates of the Prenestine Fortune, used by pagan sages in early Imperial Rome, employed letters written on wooden cubes. This form of divination was supposed to have been taught to the Etruscans by Egyptian travelers. It consisted of writing the individual letters of a person's name on individual cubes made of the wood of the laurel tree. They were thrown at random into an urn made of silver, the metal of Isis, and pulled out at random to make letter-sequences, which were then interpreted.

The Kitzbühel findings may be surviving examples of this technique. Similarly, the earliest known reference to runic divination mentions fruit-tree wood. The use of wooden slivers inscribed with divinatory signs is recorded by Tacitus in his book *Germania,* written in the year 98 A.D.:

—ɷ—

Beyond any other people, they take note of divination and casting lots. Their technique of lot-casting is simple: they cut a branch from a fruit-bearing tree and cut it into small portions. They mark these with certain signs and scatter them randomly without order over a white cloth. Then, having invoked the gods and with eyes toward the heavens, the community's priest, if the divination is public, or, if in private the father of the family, one at a time, picks up three pieces, and interprets them according to the signs previously written upon them.

—ɷ—

Tacitus does not mention the word "rune," but this is a good description of a three-rune divination, for the symbols he mentions could have been none other than runes at this period. It is possible that Tacitus's "fruit-bearing tree" was the rowan. Venantius Fortunatus, writing later, describes the same process, and uses the word *runa.*

As we can see from Tacitus and Fortunatus, since early times the runes have been bound up closely with the drawing of lots and divination in general. The actual word "rune" is still associated with an old method of land-allocation in Scotland. Villagers each had a number of strips of land in different parts of the fields around the village, known as "Run-rig," after the "runs" or lots drawn to make the allocation for each "rig" or ridge of land.

hISTORIC RUNIC INSCRIPTIONS

Historically, the various versions of the Futhark are known from several sources: actual inscriptions with all of the characters and a number are extant. In addition, various magical and dedicatory inscriptions have given us information on variants and additional runes. Archaeologically, there are several existing artifacts bearing the Elder Futhark. They come from a remarkably wide area of Europe. The earliest complete rune-row known is on an early fifth-century Gothic stone from Kylver, Gotland, Sweden. Another early and almost complete row is also from Sweden. It is inscribed on a stamped gold talisman, known as a *bracteate,* of the middle of the sixth century, from Vadstena, Östergotland. Another bracteate of the same period, from Grumpan, Scaraborgs Län, has most of the runes visible, though it is damaged. Nineteen runes remain on a stone pillar discovered at Breza, near Sarajevo, Yugoslavia, dated to the first half of the sixth century. The first 20 runes, in order, are inscribed on a silver brooch from Charnay, Burgundy, France, of the end of the sixth century. The two Swedish bracteates have the 24 runes divided by dots into groups of eight, the *ættir.* This division of the runes is an integral part of rune-lore. Each of the three ættir is ruled over by a Northern god and goddess. The first ætt, beginning with the rune Feo, is sacred to Frey and Freja; the second ætt, which commences with the rune Hagal, is ruled by Heimdall and Mordgud; and the third ætt, starting with the rune Tyr, by the god Tyr and his consort, Zisa.

Although the widely-used Elder Futhark had 24 runes, the people of Frisia found it necessary to create four additional ones, probably owing to changes in their language which necessitated new phonetic characters. This Frisian Futhark of 28 staves dates from around 550-650 A.D. There are several rune-staffs surviving from the Frisian runic era. One, which has been dated at circa 800 A.D., bore a runic spell that promised to give its possessor power over the sea's waves and tides. An important example of this 28-character rune row is inlaid in brass and silver wire upon a short sword or ceremonial knife known as *Scramasax,* now in the British Museum in London. This fascinating relic was dredged up from the bed of the River Thames in 1857. It is likely that it was cast there as an offering to the sacred tidal river, into which artifacts, especially weapons, armor and shields, had been thrown since the Bronze Age. It is believed to date from the ninth century.

On colonizing southern Britain, and creating the new country of England, people of Anglian, Saxon, and Jutish stock incorporated additional runes into the 28-rune Frisian Futhark. First, it was enlarged to 29 characters, and later, in Northumbria (the northern part of England, north of the River Humber), to 33. This was the longest coherent rune-row developed. Although other characters additional to this are known, they have not been found in full rune-rows, and their positions and meanings are uncertain. In mainland Europe and England, with the introduction of Roman-style, church-based education, the use of runes had a gradual decline. However, they were recorded in monkish writings, several of which are still in existence. They also survived in folk-magic, which included "ornament" on artifacts such as tools, musical instruments, vehicles, boats, and buildings, where they continue to be in use today.

In Scandinavia and its colonies such as Iceland, and parts of the British Isles, the runes flourished for a much longer period than elsewhere. There, the runic system was used for all types of writing, both sacred and secular. But the number of staves in the Futhark was reduced to sixteen. Most of the surviving runic inscriptions, such as the Danish, Norwegian, Swedish, and Manx memorial stones, are in this Younger Futhark. Around 2,500 rune stones survive in Sweden to this day. In this process of the reduction of the rune-row, eight of the Elder Futhark runes were abandoned. The major use of this rune-row was for inscriptions and magical formulae carved on memorial stones. Several versions of this Futhark are known, each of which differs in some significant way from the others. Each type has its own descriptive name; for example, the Gørler, Rök, mixed, and Hälsinge

Runes. The oldest record of rune names is the Abecedarium Nordmannicum (Codex 878), dating from the ninth century. This was written as the result of studies by German Christian monks including Hrabanus Maurus (780-876) and his student, Walahfrid Strabo, who was at Fulda from 827 until 829. The Abecedarium Nordmannicum contains the sixteen characters of the Danish Futhark as follows: "Feu first; Ur thereafter; Thuris the third stave; Os thereabove; Rait at the end is written; Chaion connects with Hagal; Naut has Is, Ar, and Sol; (Tyr), Bria, and Man in middle; Lagu, the light-filled; Yr ends all."

Later, in the thirteenth century, a new rune set known as the dotted runes evolved in Scandinavia from the sixteen-rune Younger Futhark. This was an expanded Futhark, which had up to 27 characters, and which, unlike all other Futharks, was written in the letter-order of the Roman alphabet. An excellent example of dotted runes is on the Saleby Stone, Skaraborgs Län, Sweden, which dates from 1228. The dotted runes marked the end of runic development, until in the early part of this century, when Guido von List developed the Armanen system of runes.

A large number of ancient Scandinavian rune stones still survive, and from them, the names of several important rune-masters, such as the Swede, Opir, and the Manxman, Gaut Björnsson, are known. But in addition to Scandinavia, the Isle of Man, and Scotland, these Norse runes were also used in Ireland. A Viking Age wooden sliver with the Younger Futhark, found in excavations of the earliest period of the city, was exhibited at the Millennium Exhibition in Dublin in 1988. Later versions of the Younger Futhark, modified so that they could be written by pen, exist in medieval Irish manuscripts. The names of the runes and their meanings were recorded around the same time in the Old English, Norwegian, and Icelandic Rune-Poems. There are also in existence several Danish runic manuscripts dating from the fourteenth and fifteenth centuries. For example, the fourteenth-century Codex Runicus, kept in Copenhagen, preserves the Skaanse Loy, the provincial laws of Skåne.

In folk magic, and on the peasant calendars known as the Rimstock or Primestave, runes continued in use until relatively recent times. Among other uses, runes have been used in heraldry; as tradesman's house-marks (the Merkelapper of Norway, many of which are preserved in the museum at Bergen); and as hunters' marks and farmers' marks (including the Norwegian Bumerker). They were used among the craftsmen's marks of medieval (and later) stone-masons, and for lot-casting in country parishes, such as Run-rig. At the present time, after the recent revival of traditional brick construction in England, one can detect the customary Ing or Odal runes in contrasting-colored brickwork.

The end of the nineteenth century saw a renewal of intellectual interest in the runes, especially from the magical viewpoint. Most important in this revival was the new eighteen rune-row of Guido von List. This he derived from the Danish-Norse mixed runes, to which he added a further two characters, based upon old runic practice. He identified each of the eighteen runes with one of the eighteen spells of Hávamál, giving each rune a magical reading. Although of modern origin, this became popular in German-speaking countries, and remains so to this day. His work led to a new awareness that the runes are something living, more than just dry antiquarian studies for scholars in the paneled rooms of ancient universities. In German-speaking countries, this new awareness was part of a "back to the roots" movement. This was connected intimately with nationalist sentiments, often couched in terms of extreme right-wing politics and their associated racist theories. This strand of propagandist rune-lore culminated in the Nazi period, with the subversion of the runes and other ancient sacred sigils as political symbols. It has taken a long time since the fall of Nazism in 1945 for some of these characters, especially the Sig and Odal runes, to be seen again in their true light as runes and not as Ahrimanic symbols of oppression or rallying-points for extremists.

RUNE MAGIC

As an esoteric system, the runes are associated with a considerable magical lore. In former times, whenever runes were inscribed on wood, bone, or stone, they were colored with pigment. This had both a utilitarian purpose (of making them visible) and a magical function. When inscribed on metal, runes were inlaid with another metal, usually silver or copper.

Esoterically, the process of coloring runes is a means of enlivening them with magic power. This tradition of painting the spirit into an object exists in cultures throughout the world. This is documented in the Norse Sagas. For example, the wise woman Thurfidr carved runes into a tree's roots, reddening them with her own blood, and signing incantations to bring the downfall of Grettir. (*Grettis Saga,* chapter 79.)

Blood was not the only coloring material used: any reddening material was acceptable. The pigment from the root of the herb madder or red ochre was used in ancient times, and red paint is used today. There are etymological connections between rune-magic and these colorings. In Old Norse, madder is *madhra,* related to the Norse name of the rune Man, *madhr.* The magical power of ochre is preserved in the East Anglian English dialect word *tiver.* This is used to describe the red ochre coloring used formerly for marking sheep, which was a remnant in country usage of the sacred ochre once used in rune-magic. In Old English, this was *teafor,* cognate with the "god" word on the Negau helmet, the Old Norse word *taufr,* and the Old High German word, *Zoubar,* magic.

Thus, in central and northern Europe, runes and magic have always gone together. There are runes and runic formulae for every eventuality. In the *Volsunga Saga,* Brunhild teaches Sigurd "runes or of other matters that are at the roots of things":

—⚡—

"Know the war runes

If you would be great!

Cut them on the hilt of the tempered sword,

Some on the brand's back,

Some on its shining side,

Twice the name Tyr there.

—⚡—

Sea-runes, good at need,

Learnt for saving ships,

For the good health of the swimming-horse;

Cut them on the stern,

Cut them on the rudder-blade,

And set flame to the planed oar;

However big the sea-hills are,

However blue below,

Hail from the main, then come home.

—⚡—

Learn well the word-runes,

If you will that no man

Pay you back for the grief you gave;

Wind these,

Weave these,

Cast them all about you,

At the Thing*

*council assembly

Where people throng
Going until the end.

—⟋⟍—

Know the wisdom of ale-runes,
If you do not want another man's wife
To seduce away a trusting heart;
Cut them on the mean-horn,
On the back of each hand,
And inscribe a Not rune upon thy nail.

—⟋⟍—

You should gather help-runes
If you want skill
To free a child from a laboring mother;
Cut them in hollow hands,
Wrapped around the joints,
Call for the good-folk's valued help.

—⟋⟍—

Learn the wisdom of the branch-runes
If you love medicine;
And want to know about healing wounds.
Score them on the bark,
On the buds of trees,
Whose branches face the east.

—⟋⟍—

You must deal with thought-runes
If you, of all people, will be
The fairest-souled being, and wisest,
These were told,
These first-cut,
These first High Hropt took to heart.

They were scratched on the shield
That stands before the shining god,
On Aarvakr's (Early-Waking's) reins,
On All-Knowing's hoof,
On the wheel that runs
Under Rögnir's chariot;
On Sleipnir's jaw-teeth,
On the sledge's traces,
On the paws of the rough bear,
And on Bragi's tongue,
On the claws of the wolf,
And the beak of the eagle,
On bloody wings,
And the bridge's end,
On loosing's palms,
And the paths of sympathy.
On glass, on gold,
On good silver,
In wine and herb,

And the witch-wife's seat;
On Gungnir's point,
And Grani's breast,
On the nail of the Norns,
And the beak of night-owl.

—⚭—

All these cut this way
Were planed off and cut up,
And mixed with sacred mean,
And sent upon the wide ways.
Some stay with the elves,
Some stay with the Esir,
Or with the wise Vanir,
Or some still remain
With the children of humankind.

—⚭—

These are the book-runes,
And the runes of good-help,
And all of the ale-runes,
And the runes of great strength:
To whoever they may assist,
Uncontaminated, unspoilt;
They are wholesome to possess:
Thrive with them, then.
When you have learnt their lore,
Until the gods end your life-days."

From this, it is clear that the runes apply to all aspects of human existence. There are special names given to runes according to the function to which they can be applied. For example, Biarg-runes (birch-runes) can be used to call on the Great Mother to assist in childbirth, and generally protect pregnant women. Malrunes (speech-runes) are for gaining recompense for injuries. In former times, they were inscribed on the posts, pillars, and seats of places where trials were held and judgment pronounced. Hogrunes (mind-runes) were written on the breast or genitals, bringing the person surpassing excellence in mental abilities. Sig-runes rendered their users skillful and crafty, with the power to obtain victory in all disputes. They were marked on the person's gloves, the hilt of his sword, his war-trumpet and other significant personal possessions. Each time the rune was inscribed, the sacred name of Thor had to be invoked twice by the ancient craft of calls known as *Galderdikt*. Troll-runes were runes used for divination, while Swart-runes were used for necromantic conjurings. Brun-runes (fountain runes) ensured the safety of seafarers. They were cut on the rudder and stern of a vessel. Lim-runes were marked on the leaves and bark of trees which inclined toward the south. Their use was to cure diseases. Ale-runes, or Alrunes, were protective against enchantment. Willu-runes were "cryptic, sepulchral, or deceitful" letters, for as part of their magic and mystery, the runes historically sometimes had a cryptic use. At times this was merely a simple encoding of a name, as in an acrostic.

A good example of this can be found in the Anglo-Saxon poem, *Elene*. Written by Cynewulf in England toward the end of the eighth century, it has the poet's name encoded cryptically by means of the rune names.

—ᚱ—

Always until then the man had been beaten by surges of sorrow; a smoldering torch (C) was he, though in the mead-hall he received treasures, apple-shaped gold. He bemoaned the evil (Y), he, the comrade of sorrow (N); he suffered

distress, cruel secret thoughts, though for him the horse (E) measured the mile-
paths, ran proudly, bedecked with ornaments. Joy (W) is lessened, and pleasure,
too, as the years pass; youth has departed and former pride. The splendor of
youth was once ours (U). Now in time, the old days have gone, the joys of life
have fled, even as water (L) glides away, like moving floods. Wealth (F) is fleeting
for all men under heaven; the adornments of the Earth vanish…

—⁓—

Thus the poem enumerates the runes Kan, Yr, Not, Ehwaz, Wunjo, Ur, Lagu, and Feo in order, spelling the author's name, Cynewulf.

But the ancient rune-masters knew more about encodement than simple name-spelling. Several surviving runic inscriptions have a series of encoded messages which still await decipherment. The longest runic inscription known in Scandinavia—760 characters—is inscribed on the Rök rune stone in Ostergotland; it has a large number of cryptic runes in different systems. Another repository of cryptic runes is inside the megalithic chambered cairn at Maeshowe, on the main island of the Orkneys. Unusually, these can be dated precisely. The Orkneying Saga records two visits to Maeshowe by seafarers. The first visit was by the crusader Rognvaldr Kali in the winter of 1151-2, when his men plundered the Neolithic burial in the tumulus, and took away the treasure there. The second visit was on January 6, 1153, when Earl Harald and his men sheltered in the now-desecrated howe during a snowstorm "…and two men among them went mad there." The stones inside Maeshowe bear 29 runic inscriptions, some of them in cryptic bind-runes. One reads, "That man most skilled in rune-craft west over the sea cut these runes." It is probable that inscriptions were made on both occasions.

There are various types of cryptic bind-runes. One of the most common is Hahalruna, or tree runes. These are numerical bind-runes based on the three ættir and the number of the rune in the ætt. The stroke or strokes to the left of the upright represent which ætt the character comes from, and those to the right represent the number corresponding with the rune in that ætt. For example, a rune with two strokes to the left and four strokes on the right represents ætt No. 2, the ætt of Hagal, and rune No. 4 in this ætt, Jera. Of course, the key to such a cipher can change; new ættir or new rune-orders could be devised to confuse the would-be reader. In addition to Halharuna or Hahalrunir, there are several other systems, including Kvistrunir, twig runes. The method of working these is the same as Hahalruna, except that the lines point upwards instead of downwards. Another system of ætt and number in that ætt is Iisrunir, where series of small and large Is ("I") runes alternate, indicating ætt and number. Similarly, Lagorunir does the same thing with Lagu runes. Stofrunir is more cryptic still, using groups of dots to signify ætt and number. In Ireland, a similar system called the Ogham of Bricriu was used, referring to the Ogham tree alphabet. There are two sorts of Tialdrunir, "tent runes." Found most notably at Rök, these are based on an "X" shape. They are read clockwise, starting at the left. One form is like the tree and twig runes, carrying "ætt and number" codes, while the other form uses each "leg" of the "X" as the stave that bears an actual rune or runes.

Finally, there are the systems of runes that did not involve writing at all. The word *Kiaprunir* describes runes "made by the simple motion of the fingers, or some other instrument," a type of semaphore. Similar techniques are known from Irish tradition as *Sron Ogham,* where letters were made by laying the fingers across the nose in appropriate ways. *Coïr Ogham* used the foot as the base, while Bar Ogham used the hand as the stem for this version of sign language. Finally, with the cryptic runes, there is the system known as *Olofrunir,* which were runes transmitted by knocks or drumbeats, a true forerunner of the Morse Code.

The Norwegian-American cryptographer Alf Monge has shown that some runic inscriptions used cryptography to encode dates. It is probable that the ancient rune-masters were the inventors of many of these systems, for the Mojbro stone in Uppland, Sweden, for example, is the earliest known use of the form of encryption known as a transposition cipher. Of course, this knowledge had a military use. The Maeshowe inscriptions were written by crusading warriors, and the use of runes as cryptography continued in the Scandinavian military tradition until the eighteenth century. For example, in 1543, Mogens Gyldenstjerne, the Danish Admiral, used runes in his private journal. During the Thirty Years' War, the Swedish General Jacob de la Gardie used them for "coded" military communications. In 1639, the runes were suppressed in Iceland as "witchcraft," the name then applied to pagan traditions which had survived. As in other parts of northern Europe, the knowledge of rune-magic had continued underground in Iceland. After 1639, possession of runes became a capital offense, and unfortunate people were burned at the stake for the ability to write in runes, which the authorities called witchcraft. This vicious law was enforced vigorously, causing much suffering. For example, in 1681, Arni Pétursson was burned at the stake in the presence of the Althing (parliament) of Iceland for the offense of using Kotruvers. These were magical spells, usually the invocation of the names of canonized Norwegian kings, written in runes on parchment, carried on the hope of winning at Kotra (backgammon).

The Riddle of Divination

In the Germanic and Norse poetic tradition, which is closely related to rune-lore, there is much use made of kennings, which are allusions used to describe something. Waves in the ocean were called "mountains of the sea," the sea itself "the fishes' bath," and fire was known as "the spoiler of twigs." These were very basic kennings, but many others were allusions to historical or mythic events. For example, gold was called "the seed of Kraki" of "the plains of Fyris" after an incident with gold that took place between the Danish King Hrólf Kraki and Aoils, king of Sweden at the Plains of Fyris. Similarly, from other sagas and legends, gold was called "the Otter's Ransom" or "Sif's Hair." Throughout Norse poetry we find allusive kennings like "the glory of Elves," meaning the sun, and "Kvasir's blood" or "Hnitbjörg's Sea," for poetry. Kennings were often adopted as proper names for objects, especially weapons. Many Norse sagas record names such as "Shield's Enemy" for a battle-ax; "Net of Spears," "Hall-roof of Odin," "Battle-Shelterer," "Sun of Odin," and "War-Linden" for shields; "Serpent of the Wound," "The Byrnie's Fear," "Torch of the Blood," "Tongue of the Scabbard," "Battle-Serpent," and "Dog of the Helmet" for swords. Runes, too, have similar kennings; for example, the rune Dorn is "Hrungnir's Heart." More complex runic kennings exist, such as the sword-name "Ice of Battle," meaning a weapon that brings stillness—death—suggestive of the quality of the rune Is, ice.

Below is a perfect example of kenning in an ancient Irish formula, Druim Suithe, which describes the sacred yew tree of Erin. Kennings are a very important means of expression, for they are words that encode a deeper, allegorical meaning, an alternative way of looking at things, just as do the runes. Druim Suithe contains descriptions of the yew tree's uses, allusions to construction, religion (both pagan and Christian), time-telling, execution, and shamanry, among others. The runic parallel of this poem is Yr. As well as to record and to entertain, the art of the bard was to encourage lateral thinking, something largely missing from modern culture. It is well demonstrated here:

—◊◊◊—

"Tree of Ross,

A king's wheel,

A prince's right,

A wave's noise,

Best of creatures,

A straight firm tree,

Door of heaven,

Strength of a building,

The good of a crow,

A word-pure man,

Full-great bounty,

The Trinity's mighty one,

A measure's hours,

A mother's god,

Mary's son,

A fruitful sea,

Beauty's honor,

A mind's lord,

Diadem of angels,

Shout of the world,

Banba's renown,

Might of victory,

> *Judgment of origin,*
> *Judicial doom,*
> *Faggot of sages,*
> *Noblest of trees,*
> *Glory of Leinster,*
> *Dearest of bushes,*
> *Vigor of life,*
> *Spell of knowledge,*
> *Tree of Ross."*

—⁓—

Closely related to poetic kennings are riddles, which challenge the listener to decipher the meaning of a kenning or metaphor. Like a kenning, a riddle is a description of something in alternative terms, suggesting something quite different but is nevertheless linked conceptually with it. An ancient Greek riddle poses this quandry: "Speak not, and thou shalt speak my name. But must thou speak? Thus again, a great marvel, in speaking thou shalt also speak my name." Answer: silence. An Anglo-Saxon riddle describes, in allegorical terms, the form and function of a human artifact: "I saw a creature in the cities of men who feeds the cattle; it has many teeth; its beak is useful; it goes pointing downward; it plunders gently and returns home; it searches through the slopes, seeking herbs; always it finds those that are not firm; it leaves the fair ones fixed by their roots, quietly standing in position, gleaming brightly, blooming and growing." Answer: a rake.

These examples are typical of the character of ancient riddles, for a well-thought-out riddle can provide a valid metaphorical description of something. Riddles and kennings emphasize resemblances and correspondences between seemingly disparate things bringing new ways of looking at the world. In his work *On Poetry*, Aristotle wrote, "The very nature indeed of a riddle is this, to describe a fact in an impossible combination of words (which cannot be done with the real names for things, but can be with their metaphorical substitutes.)" This mode of thought, now sadly neglected, is the key to a proper understanding of divination using the runes.

The meanings of the runes are riddles in this sense. Many of their concepts demonstrate the similarity between two apparently unrelated objects, processes, or concepts. In divination, this quality is most marked. In this context, it is significant that the oracles of ancient Greece and Rome often answered questions by riddles. Because they could not understand the concepts underlying kennings and riddles, opponents of oracles and divination have viewed this mode of answering as an example of incompetence or of "fudging" the issue. But this is a simplistic viewpoint which merely attempts to explain away as a triviality a tradition grounded in philosophical and psychological realities. Although riddles are now restricted almost exclusively to children in a context of entertainment, in former times they were taken seriously as a means of education in thought processes.

When conducted properly, science is the most rational of human activities. It is the pursuit of knowledge, and through knowledge, understanding. Scientific knowledge is gained from the application of the rational, linear aspects of human thought processes to observation and experimentation. But scientific experimentation can only be applied to systems where most variable criteria can be brought under the control of the experimenter. This is its major limitation; control can be achieved rarely in real-life situations.

Fortunately, linear, rational patterns of thought are not the only ones to which humans have recourse. While they are essential in most circumstances, linear, logical thought patterns seem to operate in a manner unaware of alternative connections. Riddles, kennings, and the rune-meanings provide an alternative, non-logical way of looking at things. Through the riddle of metaphor, a new idea is conveyed. When it works well, this realization comes as a startling event. It can bring a pleasant surprise, an unexpected "flash of insight." Kennings and riddles can bring new wisdom, and especially when the connection does not fit in with already-held views. They are an essential element of all divination. The riddles uttered by the ancient oracles provided the querent with new associations in the mind, new ways of looking at things, and, perhaps, a means to solve difficult problems.

Traditional society had a place for this alternative viewpoint, and the bardic tradition of ancient Britain is a good example of this. Bardism had a triadic organization, divided into three ranks or degrees: the Bards, the Druids, and the Vates (sometimes known as Ovates, Euhages, or Gutatros). While the Bards and Druids were initiates in transmitted discipleship and priesthood respectively, the bardic tradition saw the Vatis, the shamanic diviners, as necessarily outside this structure.

An ancient Welsh document, *The Privileges of Bardism,* stated that the Vates had "his degree under the privilege of genius and commendable sciences: Discipleship shall not be required in respect to him...and this is for the purpose...of improving and increasing the sciences of art, by adding everything new to them." There is no hint of conservatism or fundamentalism here. The Vates were vibrantly open to everything new, and it was their duty to gain fresh insights through divination.

Divinatory techniques are the means of access to those forces and processes which transcend linear perceptions of cause and effect. Because of this, the result of any divination can be a challenge to established ways of doing things. But, at the same time, it may be the only method that will work under the circumstances. It is not possible to have free divination under the control of dogmatism. The ancient Celtic tradition of Wales recognized that the wisdom of those schooled in the essentially conservative disciplines of academic thought was essential to the continuance of society. But it also saw that the non-rational, free elements of human experience were necessary to tackle any new problems that might arise. Problem-solving often requires methods outside one's own experience. Sometimes, the non-rational part of the psyche can provide answers to problems that logical thought cannot.

Ultimately, divination is a craft, like any other. A craft is a set of techniques designed with the intention of achieving a practical result in the physical world. The state-of-the-art in any craft is the present conclusion of the results and failures of past trial-and-error, adapted through the experience and intuition of the practitioners. It is the result of an evolutionary process which makes the craft naturally adapted to the conditions under which it is expected to operate. Thus, it is appropriate to the times in which it operates, while not rejecting the useful elements from the past—the retronuevo principle. Furthermore, any living craft assimilates the knowledge gained from scientific experiment and observation, and deals with it in the light of experience and traditional ways of doing things. It should draw from all and any sources that are advantageous to its progress. It must reject nothing on the grounds of doctrine, dogma, or politics. The laws governing the universe may or may not be constant for all time.

So our understanding of the universe is only an approximation which is more or less accurate for the time in which it is postulated. However, the principle underlying runic divination, indeed, all divination, is that all points in the continuum we call space-time are qualitatively unique. Every event associated with any point in the space-time continuum contains the quality of the moment. The unique individual quality of each point in space-time can be found by investigating its relationship to every other point in that continuum. This can be expressed in a symbolic language that is present in both nature and human consciousness. The runes form one such genuinely neutral symbolic language which enables the practitioner to determine this quality.

In the Northern Tradition, of which the runes are an integral part, the underlying, primal influence is called *örlog*. Sometimes örlog was visualized as the goddess behind fate, but more often it is seen as a principle, the eternal law of the universe, a power with no beginning and no end. Literally, the word "örlog" means "primal law." As it affects us, örlog is that assemblage of events, processes, objects, and structures which have occurred or existed in the past, whose combination and effects make the present as it is today. Örlog is sometimes translated as "fate" or "destiny," but there is no hint of predestination as the word "fate" often implies. In the Northern Tradition, destiny is ruled over symbolically by the Threefold Goddesses of fate who generally symbolize the basic triadic nature of all processes. This triadic nature exists most basically as the beginning, middle, and end of anything in time, but applies equally at many levels of existence. The Great Goddess always appears as one of her three aspects: the virgin, the mother, and the old woman. She is often depicted as the moon, which is a perfect representation of this principle, having three visible phases. The first is first quarter, which is the waxing, early phase of the moon, equivalent to the virgin. The second phase is full moon, portrayed as the mother, while the waning last quarter is the old woman. Sometimes, this imagery exists as three separate female deities: The Deac Matrones, or mothers, were important deities of the Celts. This threefold process is personified by the Three Norns, described in the Norse poem Völuspå (The Seeress's Vision):

—⚏—

Thence come the women

Who much do know;

Three from the hall

Beneath the Tree:

One they named Was,

And Being next,

The third, Shall Be.

—⚏—

The Norns are Urd, who symbolizes the past; Verdandi, the eternal present; and Skuld, that which is coming. The first of the Three Norns spins the thread of existence, passing it on to Verdandi, who weaves it into the patterns of the present, the Web of Wyrd. From her, it passes to Skuld, who rips it to shreds and disperses it to the eight winds. The Norns' actions are not arbitrary, however. They are under örlog, the eternal law of the universe, to which all beings, including the gods, are subject: past, present, and future. At a basic level, the Norns' function is to make us take heed of the lessons of the past, make good use of our present time, and be aware of future possibilities, both good and bad. Several of the runic divinations in this book are based on the principles embodied in the Three Norns.

The subject matter concerning the Norns is Wyrd. In Old Saxon, Wyrd is called *Wurd,* and in Old German, *Wurt.* In Iceland, Wyrd was known as *Urdr,* the first Norn. All of these names are derived from an archaic Indo-European verb meaning "to become," the German *werden.* In the Scots dialect of English, "weird" can mean a "fateful being; a dealer in the supernatural; a prediction or prophecy." As a verb, it also can mean "to doom something to; to predict; to send good wishes to someone magically; or to make something liable." Here, the meaning of Wyrd can be translated roughly as "destiny." More properly, it is the result of the history and relationships that determine someone's or something's place or status at the present time. Naturally, the potential range of events which can occur in relation to this thing or person are limited by the conditions under which they exist. These constraints and possibilities are their Wyrd. The forces which produced this Wyrd are their örlog.

Human beings have free will. But there are constraints on that free will which, in combination with the acts caused by the will, result in the experiences, happenings, and events of one's life. This is our Wyrd, the particular combination of circumstances and processes that we inherit as the result of örlog.

Symbolically, this Wyrd can be envisioned as a web, a sort of woven material composed of myriad strands or threads. This was the ancient viewpoint of Wyrd, recorded in the Old English expression "woven by the decrees of fate." The Norn's web is said to be so large that it stretches from the mountains in the East to the ocean in the West. The color of their threads depends upon the nature of the events about to occur. For example, a black thread, woven into the web from north to south, was considered an omen of impending death.

In the classical tradition, the Wyrd-weaving Norns are paralleled by the Three Fates, sometimes known collectively by their Greek name of *Moirai,* or the Latin *Parcae.* The three Greek Moirai, Clotho, Lachesis, and Atropos, were seen as daughters of night. *Moira* means "part," and, according to the Orphic tradition, their number (three) corresponds to the "parts" or phases of the moon. Clotho parallels Urd, Lachesis is the equivalent of Verdandi, and Atropos is identified with Skuld. In traditional representations of the Fates, Clotho holds a distaff, Lachesis has a spindle, and Atropos uses her shears to cut the thread of life. Clotho spins the thread, and Lachesis measures it. As the Parcae, these goddesses are None, Decima, and Morta, who have, respectively, the same functions as the Moirai. Their names mean "nine," "ten," and "death." The three Moirai and Percae are allied closely to the Three Graces of classical tradition: Aglaia, Euphrosyne, and Thalia. These three female figures represent the three phases of the process of love: beauty, arousing desire, leading to fulfillment. Another aspect of the Graces is as the triadic aspect of generosity, the giving, receiving, and reciprocating of gifts. In this regard, they signify the essential aspect of the rune Gebo. In Celtic tradition, these triadic fates and graces are symbolized by the Matrones, otherwise known as "the mothers." In Wales, the fairies are known still as "the mothers." Celtic and Romano-Celtic images of three women, often identical to one another, can be seen in many museums in the countries of northern and central Europe.

The Mothers are usually shown as three women bearing fruit or cornucopias. Surviving inscriptions emphasize their nature as fertility deities, providers of abundance. Here, they reflect one aspect of the Roman Parcae, whose name is connected with the Latin word *parere,* "to bring forth." In the Old English calendar, December 25 was called Modranect, "The Night of the Mothers," after these goddesses, aspects of the Great Goddess. They were also seen as aspects of the three Fates. Around 1200, Saxo Grammaticus wrote that in his time, the pagans consulted the Threefold Goddesses about their children's futures. At the sanctuary of the Goddess, three priestesses spoke for Her: "three maidens sitting on three seats."

In English tradition, these three Fates or Norns were known as "The Wierd Sisters." Although attempts were made by the Christian church, the knowledge and veneration of these sisters was not suppressed in England. Around 1190, Bartholomew of Exeter recommended two years' penance for any woman "who lays a table with three knives for the service of the Fates in order that they may bring a good future to those who are born there." Geoffrey Chaucer, writing around 1385, wrote in *The Legend of Good Women* of "the Werdys that we clepen Destiné" ("the Wyrds that we call destiny"). Also, *The Court of Love,* written around 1450, states, "I mene the three of fatall destiné that be our Werdes." ("I mean the three of fatal destiny that be our Wyrds"). Later, the Threefold Goddess was the model for the three witches in William Shakespeare's *Macbeth,* where they foretell the downfall of the usurping Scots king. Shakespeare took the story from the 1577 *Chronicle of Holinshed,* who described them as "three women in wild apparel resembling creatures from an elder world." Further on in the work, Holinshed states that these were none other than the "Wierd Sisters, that is the goddesses of destinie." Holinshed's use of the words "elder world" have the meaning of eldrich, "unearthly." Even today, the modern pagan tradition is sometimes referred to as the "elder" faith, meaning both older and pre-Christian."

The all-pervasive ancient triadic view of the world symbolized by the Threefold Goddess of past-present-future is best preserved from the Celtic branch of the Northern Tradition. There, the esoteric cosmology enshrined in the Welsh bardic tradition is based upon this eternal threefold. It is manifested in many ways. According to the ancient text known as *Barddas,* existence has a triadic nature: "The three materials of every being and existence, calas, and hence every motionless body and solidity; fluidity, and hence every cessation, migration, and return; and nwyvre, hence every animation and life, and every understanding and knowledge." This last quality, *nwyvre,* is the Celtic name for "breath of life" known in every traditional, shamanic view of the world. It is the Norse *önd;* the *pneuma* of the Greeks; the *prana* of India; the *qi* of China; the *ki* of Japan; the rainbow serpent of the native Australians; and the *od* of Von Reichenbach. Many esoteric writers have equated this "energy" with the divine principle which pervades all things. Today, the "earth dragon," known in France as the *voivre* and in England as the *wyvern,* is portrayed as a winged, dragon-like beast with ears, only one pair of (front) legs, and a serpent-like tail. It represents the animated "personification" of this mysterious life force.

The humanly accessible states of existence of the bardic tradition are threefold. Our abode, the earth, stands at the mid-point of the cosmic axis. This is Middle Earth (the Welsh Abred and the Norse Midgard). Lying above the earth in spiritual terms is Gwynvyd. This name translates as the "white land," and is described as the place of divine beings and humans who have ascended spiritually. This parallels the Asgard of the Norse tradition, the abode of the gods. Lying below Abred is the underworld, known in the triads as Annwn, which translates as "the abyss." Annwn is the incorporeal netherworld, from which issue lower, unpurified, spiritual forms. It is the place into which the unrighteous must descend for repurification as a preparation for their rebirth into Abred. Above, and completely external to this triad of "circles of existence," is Ceugant, the place of the unknowable and ineffable One. But this is considered outside existence, and hence not part of the triadic description of things.

Norse legend and lore abounds with triads. Archaic northern European religion recognized three divinities, two of whom were absorbed later into the Norse pantheon. They were deities of the primal forces of the Earth: Egir, the sea; Kari, the air; and Loge, fire. There were three colors recognized, visible in the rainbow: green, blue, and red, equivalent to water, air, and fire respectively. Later Norse belief divided the gods into three groups: the earlier hunter/gatherer period deities known as the Vanie; the agricultural/warrior deities, the Esir; and those who were outside either grouping, earlier divinities, allied with the Giants. In the Norse creation-myth, the first humans, Ask and Embla, were given a triadic nature by three gods. Odin gave the soul; Hoenir, the senses and the power of movement; while Lodur gave the blood and complexion. When the Fenris-Wolf was bound (see the entry for the rune Tyr), three fetters were needed before he was captive. In Norse pagan religious observance, the year was punctuated by three major festivals known as Blót. These were Vinternatsblót, on October 14, celebrating the beginning of winter; Midvintersblót, on January 14, promising peace and good harvest in the coming year; and Sommerblót, on April 14, for success in summer undertakings.

The power ascribed to the number nine is considered especially magical. A common Northern Tradition incantation is "by the power of three times three," and the number nine is very significant in Norse cosmology. There are nine worlds mentioned in the Poetic Edda, nine heavens. In ascending order, these are: Hreggmimir, Andlangr, Vidbláinn, Vidfedmir, Hrododr, Hlyrnir, Gimir, Vetrmimir, and Skatyrnir. These can be equated with the planetary spheres of classical astrology. There are also nine Valkyries, "the choosers of the slain," who take to Asgard the souls of those who have died valiantly. But however it is manifested, this triadic view of things is at the root of the runic world view, and underlies the principles and many of the techniques of runic divination, as described in Part III.

PART II
THE RUNES

Today, runes are used primarily in divination. Because of this, their individual meanings are commonly emphasized, while their use as an alphabet is played down. But, just like the Roman alphabet, in which this book is set, each of the runes has a phonetic equivalent. This enables us to use the runic system for writing, as it was used in the past. But, unlike words written in the Roman alphabet, those written in runic are composed of the combinations of meanings inherent in the runes. This is especially important in names. There are two ways to form runic names. Firstly, there is a name composed of specific runes, as in the example of Cynewulf in the previous section. But there are also names composed of rune-names. This practice was popular in Anglo-Saxon England, when several of the pagan kings had names which reflected their status, combining a rune's quality with a word for "ruler," such as Cenric ("wise king").

The phonetic value of the runes is as follows: Feo, f; Ur, u; Dorn, d, od, or th; As, a; Rit, r; Kan, k or r; Gebo, g; Wunjo, w or v; Hagal, h; Not, n; Is, i; Jera, i; Eihwaz, eo; Peorth, o; Eiwaz, x or z; Sig, s; Tyr, t; Bar, b; Ehwaz, e; Man, m; Lagu, l; Ing, ng; Odal, o; Dag, d; and Yr, y. However, the main function of this book is to describe the meaning and significance of the individual runes, and their use in divination. The major part of this section describes The Haindl Rune Oracle cards with their corresponding runes one by one in their customary order, beginning with Feo and ending with Yr, the 25th rune.

FEO

Old German, Fehu; Gothic, Faihu; Anglo-Saxon, Feoh; Old Norse, Fé.

The Feo card represents nature tamed by human agency for human benefit. It is springtime. In the foreground rises a freshly-cut tree trunk with two pruned branches, which stands like a hand held protectively in front of the landscape. The branches face toward our right, like antennae toward the conscious side of things. All is in order, under conscious human control for human benefit. In the distance, the sky is reddened by the fiery glow of the sun or a distant fire. Fire has been tamed and banished. Here, like the tree, it is under human control. The herb connected with this rune, the stinging nettle, is painful to humans through its stinging, fiery poison, yet it can be used also as a vegetable rich in vitamins and minerals, symbolizing the two-sided nature of all things.

The first rune in all runic systems, including the Elder Futhark, is Feo. Feo is the ruling rune of the first group of eight runes known as an ætt, of which there are three in the 24-character Elder Futhark. All versions of the rune name Feo have the meaning of "cow" or "cattle." This meaning is found also describing the first letter of the alphabet in the Greek and Hebrew systems, Alpha and Aleph. Symbolically, this rune signifies movable, negotiable wealth, described in the manner of traditional, pre-monetary society in terms of "cattle," valuable animals tamed for human use. Before the invention of money, an individual's wealth and status in society were measured by how many heads of cattle he owned. The runes, dating from such an archaic period, denote qualities expressed in terms of the cultural standards of the age in which they originated. But these expressed qualities are timeless. Feo makes the distinction between negotiable and non-negotiable property. Although the individual, family, or clan could not sell or barter their ancestral homestead, cattle were negotiable. Even today, in certain parts of Africa, cattle are still the measure of a person's wealth. But by the period when the runes were coming into use, this early concept of wealth as livestock had been widened to include many other valuable things under human control, and Feo was understood on a symbolic rather than a figurative level.

The cow plays a crucial role in the creation of legends of northern Europe. Northern mythology tells of the primal cow, Audhumla, which, in the early days of the world, licked a crystalline block of salt. From out of this block emerged a being known as Buri, who became the progenitor of human beings. Symbolically, Feo is the archetypal agency of energy and form from which human beings originate. In Irish tradition, this power is associated with the cow-goddess Boann. On a physical level, this refers to prehistoric European society's human dependency upon the cow for milk, meat, and hide, and the power of the ox for transportation and plowing the earth.

Symbolically, the rune Feo signifies the accumulation of conscious power and control, which often is taken as referring to money and associated matters. Even today, in the English language, the word "fee" means "payment," and *feegarrie* is the Scottish word for "expensive, showy jewelry." The accumulation of power and control can be understood in terms of the herd. Control can be exercised directly on the herd of cattle by physically moving it around. Control is also manifested through possession, exploitation, and disposal. But however it is exercised, this control is a result of will. Wild things must be tamed, whether they be animals, land, fire, or human will. In agriculture and horticulture, control is exercised in planting, tending, harvesting, and pruning. Cultivation is necessary for wealth to be reaped at harvest-time. Generally, once we possess anything, we have also to assume the responsibilities of ownership. To own and superintend anything wisely and responsibly entails correct management. Negligence, wastefulness, or avarice will soon cause failure and our downfall through the internal disintegration of the enterprise, or through personal squabbles with others. As with all things, there are two sides to wealth.

The Old English Rune Poem, which is believed to date back to the eighth century, expresses these two polar aspects of wealth: "Wealth is a comfort to everybody, yet we all must give it away freely, if we want to gain favor in the sight of the Lord." Similarly, the later Norwegian Rune Poem deals with the problems, rather than the benefits, of wealth: "Wealth causes friction between relatives, while the wolf lurks in the woods."

Because greed, avarice, and consequent envy can be the result of wealth, the possessor of wealth needs to handle it carefully and wisely in order to remain in harmony with his or her relatives and neighbors. If misused, wealth can divide families, friends, and society at large, with disastrous results. The symbolism of the ox powering the plow is relevant here: profits ought to be "plowed back" into society for the benefit of all, for one may only reap next autumn's harvest by sowing last year's grain, not by hoarding it. The ox can only plow a straight furrow if human supervision is unwavering, requiring the exercise of the human will.

Throughout the runic Futhark we can find this call for the maintenance of order sustained by responsible actions. Here, the Old English Rune Poem recommends non-attachment to wealth. The accumulation of wealth should not be regarded as an end in itself, for it is divisive to society and leads to conflict. Runic wisdom teaches that materialism can become a burden rather than a liberator. In modern terms, Feo refers to money in general, but more specifically, the ability or chance to gain worldly success and great wealth, and to keep it. On an esoteric level, this rune signifies spiritual wealth. Like material wealth, spiritual wealth—the inner teachings and wisdom of religious systems—should not be hoarded by priesthoods and self-appointed "gurus," but should be given away freely to all sincere seekers of the truth.

In its correspondence with the cards of the tarot, Feo is equated with trump I, The Magician. The manipulation of power, the business of the magician, is an important aspect of the rune Feo. Here, Feo is the rune of eternal becoming, the primal force of mobile power in all of its aspects, both physical and magical. Because of its fundamentally creative nature, Feo is ascribed a female polarity, ruling the elements of fire and earth. The divinities connected with this first rune are the twin brother and sister, Frey and Freyja, bestowers of fertility and fecundity in livestock and humans. The Irish goddess Boann is a Celtic parallel of Freyja. Most importantly, the goddess Fulla is connected with this rune. A divine handmaiden of the goddess Frigg, Fulla is the keeper of her casket of jewels, and on a more general level, is a symbol of the fullness of the earth. Fulla was worshipped in Germany under the name of Abundia or Abundantia, the goddess of abundance. The cornucopia, or horn of plenty, traditionally depicted as a horn of the steer overflowing with the fruits of the earth, is the symbol of Abundia. It signifies the earth element. Esoterically, she represents the power of Feo, the ability to take power from the world and to direct it through the will into manifestation. Feo's fecund nature is reflected by its rulership of the time period from June 29 until July 14.

The major divinatory interpretation of this rune, and fifteen others in the Futhark, depends on its orientation. Any rune card can appear upright, in which case the full original meaning of the rune is present. It can also appear inverted. In most cases, this indicates that the meaning on the card is reversed.

When the rune card Feo falls upright, it indicates gain through personal effort. It tells us that if we continue to proceed along the path which we have already chosen, then the outcome of our undertaking will be successful. In a reading, an upright Feo card signifies that the querent will overcome any obstacles or opposition which may appear in the way of achieving one's goals. Feo tells us to "keep on keeping on," that our striving will be successful, even against the odds. Feo is a rune of overcoming obstacles through perseverance rather than devious strategy. Because Feo means "wealth," the upright rune indicates that the querent will gain money. But this will be earned income, wealth obtained through work, not through inheritance or as a gift.

Feo's message is basically one of positive endurance, that the querent should keep on course, and not start anything new. It is favorable for preservation of existing forms, indicating that we should conserve or consolidate our reserves. When this card is at a significant point in a reading, then it is certainly not favorable for new beginnings. Feo upright indicates that things one has planned, but not yet started, should be held in abeyance until a more favorable time. Intelligent control of the present situation and careful management are the best strategies for success.

On the emotional level, Feo indicates romantic "success" in uncertain circumstances, as, for instance, where there is a rival for a loved one's affections. This is the power of the goddess Lofn, like Fulla, another divine handmaiden of Frigg. Lofn's task is to remove all obstacles that might come in the way of lovers. In an answer to a spiritual question, Fa indicates that the querent should continue on his or her spiritual pathway, whatever the apparent hardships might be at the present. Perseverance will bring spiritual riches, the mastery of one's own true will.

Inverted, this rune card signifies a reversal of the qualities inferred from its upright form. With Feo, these reversals indicate failure or loss in one's undertakings if the course which one has already chosen to take is not changed. More specifically, the inverted Feo rune indicates monetary difficulties which may range from cash-flow problems at the least serious end to bankruptcy at the most. On a wider level, the inverted rune signifies a loss of personal influence and power, and likely failure of an undertaking that has already been started. Opposition to the querent is too powerful to be overcome, despite strenuous efforts. Weakness and indecision are indicated. One's power may also be used for destructive ends, either consciously or by default.

On a personal level, inverted Feo signifies possible emotional problems if things are allowed to continue in the same way. These may involve arguments within a relationship, leading to serious and seemingly irreconcilable disagreements. Finally, they may produce a general disharmony which can lead to intransigence from both parties and a break-up of relationships. Financial loss is indicated here, too, perhaps in the form of legal expenses or a costly divorce settlement. One meaning of the Scots word *fee* is "predestined," referring, evidently, to the inverted rune. Spiritually, it indicates that we must change our ways, whether this is interpreted as an alteration in beliefs or practices, or as a change in attitudes toward life. Not to change at such a juncture will lead to spiritual impoverishment.

UR

Old German, Uruz; Gothic, Urus; Anglo-Saxon and Old Norse, Ur.

The second rune is called Ur. Its card expresses the raw power of more primitive days, where the shape of the rune is reflected by the most archaic architecture. This is seen in the shape of the dolmens of prehistoric Europe, whose stones show little evidence of human alteration from their primal, natural condition. In all runic versions except the Old Norse, this rune signifies the primeval strength represented by the now-extinct European wild cattle known as the *urus* or *aurochs, bos primigenius.* The moon is shrouded by clouds, while the aurochs stand like ancient monuments themselves in the primal landscape, illuminated by the first rays of the sun. The Old English Rune Poem treats it thus: "The aurochs is bold with horns rising high, a fierce horn-fighter who stamps across the moors, a striking animal!" Formerly widespread in Northern and Central Europe, the aurochs was the veritable primal ox. The traditional hunting clans of ancient Northern and Central Europe held the aurochs in the same place of importance and reverence as the bison was in the life and lore of the native tribes of North America. The aurochs, however, was not totally tameless, for it was domesticated in Switzerland during the Neolithic era. Tragically, this magnificent species is extinct now; the last aurochs was killed during a hunt in Poland in 1627.

In contrast to the power of property under the individual will, expressed by the rune Feo, Ur is the raw, boundless, primal power behind creativity. It expresses the untamed qualities of primitive, archaic times. Like the attribute of the aurochs, Ur represents unmitigated strength, vital stamina, and perseverance united behind the creative potential. It is the will to struggle on against all odds, the ability to take on all comers. Ur is that power which can never come under the control of a single individual. When applied to the human realm, it is power in the collective sense, "our" power, which, if applied properly, is an irresistible bastion against tyranny. Ur is thus the rune of freedom, the condition of having sufficient internal and collective strength to be dominated by no one. Ur's influence is in the direction of good fortune. When it signifies personal success, it is a form of success which is not obtained at the expense of others. Primarily, the success of Ur is that which promotes the common good. It is the formative power, shaping and fashioning of events through the conscious will. It is the energy that upwells from the earth, as in a spring of water, that potential energy which can be felt tangibly before it manifests physically. Because of this, Ur is a rune of good physical condition, general health in body, mind, and spirit. Spiritual healing can be accomplished through the power of this rune by tapping the surprisingly powerful source of creative energy that we all have within us.

The shape of the rune Ur represents the horns of the ox, although the aurochs itself had long curving horns of which the basal portions lay in a straight line over the top of the skull. In former times, the horns of the aurochs were prized as drinking vessels fit for heroes. Traditionally an aurochs' horn could hold one gallon of ale. Aurochs' horns have been found among the grave-goods accompanying ancient warriors. In many traditions, horns are a symbol of sacredness, and the wearing of horns by shamans and saints is recognized as being a symbol of this communion with divine forces. The horned gods of pagan tradition, such as Cernunnos and Pan, are also symbols of the male generative force inherent in Ur.

Ur is ruled by the god Thor and by Urd, the first and eldest Norn, whose name means "ancient" or "primal," or, more precisely, "that which was." She signifies those events and forces which have existed in the past and which have given rise to the present condition in which we find ourselves. When it signifies healing, Ur is sacred to the Norse goddess of medicine, Eir, and her Celtic counterpart, Airmed. The medical practitioners of ancient Northern Europe were almost exclusively female, and so are the divine rulers of the craft.

Following Feo, Ur is another summertime rune, ruling the period from the 14th until the 29th of July. In the Scots dialect of English, *ure* refers to the summer heat haze, often colored by sunbeams, and the suffocating heat which goes with it. Similarly, the Old Norse interpretation of Ur has no connection with the Aurochs. Its literal meaning is "drizzle," the fertilizing mist of fine rain, which can also refer to consecrated water from a holy well sprinkled over people by a priestess or healer. The well of Urd, at which the Norns sit and spin people's fates, connected geomantically with the energy of the earth. This energy, known in the Northern Tradition as *önd,* and more specifically, personified as the nwyvre or vouivre, are the magnetic eddies and currents within the Earth over which, it is believed, the ancient geomants located standing stones and other sacred structures. Thor, as god of thunder and lightning, is the divine personification of this energy which links the earthly with the heavenly.

In the tarot, Ur parallels the trump The High Priestess, who signifies hidden influences at work and formative forces. In traditional representations, the high priestess sits between the two pillars of the Temple, Boaz and Joachin, which symbolize the two life principles. Here, the horns of the aurochs, one of which is long and one of which is short, have the same meaning. Appropriately, the rune's element is earth with a male polarity.

When the card of Ur comes upright in a runecast, then it is a fortunate reading. Ur signifies that the querent will have the freedom to do what he or she wants, with the ability to summon and use strength to overcome any difficulties which may arise. Anything requiring tenacity, will power, and stamina will be tackled successfully. Any project that the querent is involved with will be accomplished successfully, but only through hard work and a strong will. Although things will go well, the task will not be easy. The querent must learn to be self-reliant in order to progress.

Generally, Ur indicates good fortune when the reading is concerning employment, career advancement. If the hidden influences at work are tending toward change in the querent's life, indicated by other cards in the reading, then Ur signifies that the querent will have the strength and ability to cope with it. When a reading concerns health, good health and vitality are indicated. Ur can represent the active or male side of a sexual relationship: strong, passionate, and virile.

When inverted in a reading, the Ur rune signifies a failure of creativity. This may result from lethargy, having insufficient energy to carry a project through to successful conclusion. Generally, stagnation is indicated. An upside-down Ur may indicate that negative influences are acting upon the circumstances, leading to missed opportunities and general "bad luck." The querent is likely to miss an opportunity if appropriate action is not taken immediately. In combination with a rune of transition or change, such as Rit, Ehwaz, or Lagu, then an inverted Ur card indicates that the querent should allow the opportunity to pass without taking it up. The inverted card can also indicate that a drastic change in circumstances is imminent, perhaps occasioned by illness. On a social level, Ur inverted indicates a loss of positive co-operative powers, perhaps manifested as anti-social activities such as hooliganism, or worse situations like mob rule and uncontrollable riot, affecting the querent in a negative way.

ÐORN

The third rune is Dorn whose form expresses all aspects of the three-fold. The rune card for Dorn expresses the triadic nature of life: the triangular stave represents the body; the light within it, the soul; and the air around it, the mind. The red light of the soul at the center is defended and protected by the thorn enclosure. White light reflects from the black thorns of the triangular garland, whose thorns face toward the right, the direction of the conscious mind. Behind and below the rune, the vegetation culminating on the right-hand side with the ears of corn signify the season of the Lammastide harvest with which this rune is associated.

The Old German meaning of the rune is "the strong one," paralleled by the Old Norse, meaning "giant." The Gothic version means "the good one," while in the Anglo-Saxon version, it means "thorn." Whatever its name, this rune signifies resistance and protection, manifested as the resistant qualities of thorn trees, and the strength of the legendary giant known as Thurs.

The rune Dorn is sacred to the thunder god Thor. It encapsulates the awesome power of Thor's sacred weapon, the hammer Mjölnir. Dorn is thus that power which resists all that threatens to disrupt the natural order of things.

On the plant, the thorn is a protective structure which deters animals and people from coming too close. Upright, the rune Dorn represents active defense, the action of the conscious mind; while inverted, it signifies passive defense, the unconscious. When it operates passively, its effect is most often deterring. More generally, the thorn is the power of small things to inflict injury on those who would choose to challenge or attack them. The first two runes, Feo and Ur, represent the strength of tame and wild cattle respectively, but the third, Dor, exercises its power in another, but no less effective, way.

The indigenous Northern European thorn trees referred to by the rune's name are the hawthorn, the blackthorn, and the bramble. Hedges composed of the sacred thorn plants are the traditional enclosure for the sacred places of the Northern Tradition. It is still possible to find these ancient thorn-ringed sacred enclosures in Wales, where they are known as *llan*. Some enclose an ancient church which replaced an earlier Celtic shrine. The thorn plants not only protect the sacred ground from the intrusion of animals, but also prevent the entry of evil spirits. The spirit within is protected by the thorn enclosure, which acts as a boundary between the inner and the outer worlds. Before they were uprooted and obliterated to allow for modern agricultural techniques, thorn hedges surrounded every field in England, protecting the growing wheat and barley from attack by animals kept in adjacent fields. According to the Old English Rune Poem: "The thorn is very sharp, an evil thing to grip upon, very painful for anybody who falls among them," a fitting protection for a sacred place. In the East Anglian magical tradition of England, the sprite flail, composed of nine lengths of bramble, is used to purify areas before ceremonies.

The triangular form of Dorn as a symbol of sacred protection is reflected also in the former holy island of Thorney in London, upon which stand the Houses of Parliament, seat of the British government, and Westminster Abbey, crowning-place of kings and queens. Named "The Island of Thorn," the island was triangular in form, being defined by a delta of the stream known as Tyburn (Tyr's stream). As a magic island, Thorney was the site of supernatural events, including spirit lights at the consecration of the original Westminster Abbey in the seventh century. In the hereditary pagan tradition of Wiltshire, in the south of England, the triangle symbolizes the link between the three states of existence: the realm of elves and humans, the realm of animals, and the realm of plants. Each of the three points of the triangle symbolizes one of the three Lords of Life.

Dorn is the form of the pyramid, the magically-protective shape for the receptacle of the dead, paralleling the form of the conical burial mounds of prehistoric Northern Europe. Another defensive use of the Dorn-shaped triangle was in the battle formation used in Viking times, known as the *keil*. It was used by the northern martial arts warriors, dedicated to their tutelary beast, the boar, who went under the name of Svinfylking. These warriors gained entry to the enemy line in a wedge formation, as the apex of which were two warriors skilled in axe-fighting. Together, these two fighters were called *rani*, "the snout." This formidable attacking formation, also known as the "boar's throng," is associated in Northern Tradition astronomy with the constellation better known as the Pleiades. Magically, Dorn is one of the "war fetter" runes, used in binding magic for disrupting the activities of opponents, and reflecting back harmful energies onto their originators. A kenning for the rune is recorded in Snorri Sturlson's *Poetic Diction:* "Hrungnir's heart is famous. It was of hard stone and sharp-edged and three cornered like the runic stave known as 'Hrungnir's Heart' which has been made that way ever since." Hrungnir was the strongest giant, who, nevertheless, was slain by Thor. He may be equated with the name "Thurs," sometimes ascribed to this rune.

Dorn is the rune of the harvesters, especially the grain harvest at Lammastide (August 1), which is the time period ruled over by this rune (July 29 until August 13). As a musical instrument, the triangle of Dorn is an attribute of the muse Erato, patroness of lyric and love poetry. This connection in classical tradition highlights the sexual elements of Dorn, which can represent the phallus. Like Ur, Dorn signifies the masculine creative energy, the willful direction of the generative principle. Dorn can also signify regeneration. The yule-trees of "paradise," made in Bavaria and other lands, and signifying the continuance of fertility and harvests, are made of apples joined by sticks bearing vegetation and candles, having the triangular geometry of Dorn. Its element is fire, the light within the triangle, signifying the all-seeing eye of Odin, and its polarity is male.

Like the first two runes, Dorn is invertible. When upright, Dorn signifies good fortune, with additional assistance and protection in one's undertakings. It can indicate that the querent might soon receive an unexpected stroke of good luck. In this, Dorn denotes that the querent possesses the quality of being present at the right place at the right time. Dorn affords extremely powerful and auspicious protection when it occurs in a rune card reading along with the "magic" defensive runes Eoh, Eiwaz, or Yr. Upright, Dorn indicates a change of fortune for the better, the arrival of good news, or the immediate requirement that an important and perhaps far-reaching decision should be made.

Unlike most of the invertible runes, when reversed, the Dorn rune has a similar meaning to when it is upright. However, when the card is this way around, it indicates that unconscious rather than conscious factors are in operation. When in conjunction with Hagal, Not, or Is, the runes of constraint and binding, Dorn can signify potential or actual blockages in one's progress, inhibiting forces in action. In this circumstance, Dorn tells us to examine the situation critically, consolidate our position, and protect ourselves in whichever ways are appropriate. It is a warning not to over-stretch one's resources, not to test events beyond the limits of possibility of success, which at the present time is severely limited. In a career context, the querent my be countered by stronger opponents, even seeing subordinates as a threat. But, when in conjunction with other runes indicating movement and change, such as Rit, Dorn also indicates that there may be potentially disastrous results from following the present course of action without deviation. Here, it tells the querent that she or he must make changes—now! The querent should not make decisions without expert assistance. Through stubbornness, however, one may find difficulty in taking advice from others better qualified to judge the situation, becoming overprotective of one's interests and irrationally suspicious of other people's motives. It is likely that the tide of luck is running against the querent, and therefore they must be very careful in their actions. Other runes in the reading may indicate ways and means of dealing with these problems.

ᚨS

The fourth rune of the Elder Futhark is As, also known as Esc, Asa, Ansuz, or, in a variant form, as Os. The card representing As symbolizes the rainbow connection to Asgard, the dwelling-place of the Esir. The active power of divinity is expressed by the angular forms of this rainbow rune, behind which flows a warm light from behind the clouds. The rainbow's rays rise up from the left, and turn downwards again to the right into the blue void. The apices point upwards toward the gods. Here, the rainbow rune is the connection between the goddess Mother Earth, and the heavenly God of Light.

Whatever its transliteration (Esc, Asa, Ansuz, Os), this powerful rune signifies God, the divine force in action. The Icelandic Rune Poem refers to the "prince of Asgard and lord of Valhalla," Odin as the Allfather. The rune can be traced back to a most archaic period of the Indo-European tradition, where it manifested in Sanskrit as the primal sound. The primal sound, it is said, was that formative energy which triggered off the coming into being of this cycle of the universe. As is the rune of the cosmic breath, the force is known in the Northern Tradition as *önd*. This is the subtle energy known in other traditions as *pneuma, prana, ch'i, vril,* and *od.* As is the cosmic great; it is the energy, emanating from the divine source, which underlies all manifestation. Microcosmically, it signifies the divine source within the self, the individual's spiritual center.

The Anglo-Saxon version of this rune symbolizes the ash tree, which is one of the most sacred trees in the Northern Tradition. Each ash tree is a microcosmic example of the cosmic axis, the central world tree Yggdrassil. The black buds and horseshoe-shaped leaf scars of the tree account for its dedication to the god Odin and the goddess of spring, Ostara or Eostre. As the cosmic axis, As controls the maintenance of order in the cosmos. As the Old English Rune Poem tells us, "the ash, beloved of humans, towers high. In a firm position it holds well to its place, though many enemies come forward to fight it."

As the world ash, As appears as a rune of stability, maintained consciously by the divine power in the shape of the Esir, guardians of order within the universe. As is a rune of sound, more specifically in speech as intelligent communication. Although this part of its meaning was split from As by the Anglo-Saxons, and attributed to a new rune, Os, in the Elder Futhark, upon which these cards are based, this aspect is really part of As. Of Os, the Old English Rune Poem states: "The mouth is the origin of all speech, Supporter of wisdom and counselors' comfort, and a blessing and confidence to everyone." As is a rune of unfettering, as explained in the fourth spell of Hávamál: "I know the fourth one: It can liberate me rapidly if enemies bind me fast with strong chains; a call that makes bonds spring from the feet, manacles burst from the hands." As thus represents the rune of liberation of the mind through the possession of knowledge, and the wisdom to use it correctly.

As is primarily a rune of consciousness, and the order which emerges from it. It is therefore associated with the red and white fly agaric mushroom, whose qualities of access to the unconscious were well known in the past to shamans and witches. This fungus contains psychotropic substances which can produce hallucinations and physical sensations such as the feeling that one is flying. However, it is not recommended that readers should use this fungus, as it is quite possible to take a fatal dose. Whether obtained by the use of wortcunning, or by spiritual exercises such as the runic meditations known as *Galor* or *Galdardikt* (calls, the equivalent of the Oriental mantras), the power of *ódhr* (inspiration) can be obtained through the rune As. Appropriately, the corresponding element of As is air, and its polarity male. Its tutelary god is the wind god Odin, the mercurial master of shamans, education, and communication in general. As thus rules sacred songs, magical incantations, and Galdardikt. In the Norwegian Rune Poem, the equivalent rune is *óss*, meaning "the mouth of a river." Here, it is a rune of communication and the lesser merging with the greater. In the runic year cycle, As covers the early autumnal period from August 13-29.

Upright in a divination, the As rune card indicates honesty and straightforwardness. If the querent asks for it, he or she will receive unbiased, fair advice. As indicates that the querent may receive much-needed assistance from a teacher, a superior in the querent's trade or profession, or a spiritual master. This assistance will bring advancement through the creation of intellectual order. Success in taking a test or examination is indicated. According to the question asked, As can indicate favorable outcomes in connection with communications, which might mean a visit from a relative or parent, or something to do with inheritance. In general, As refers to spiritual gifts, the power of using wisely one's *önd* and *ódhr,* which make up one's *megin.*

Reversed As may signify false counsel. People who appear as advisors may actually be acting in their own best interest, not that of the querent, so caution is advised when dealing with others, even close associates. This unreliability of associates may be manifested as unreliable work and overcharging for a job. It may also come to light as dishonest advice, trickery, falsehood, and fraudulent dealings, and

travel. Rit therefore generally represents the transmutation of energies. This can take place as a transference from one place or state to another of spirit, matter, or information. Spiritually, there is the emphasis on personal transformation. The Old English Rune Poem gives the following reading for this rune: "Riding is soft for a hero inside the hall, but is more strenuous when he is astride a great horse riding the long-mile roads." Here, Rit signifies two types of "riding": horsemanship and sexual intercourse.

Esoterically, Rit stands for our conscious contact with the many disparate factors which compose our individual Wyrd. This contact can be made through the positive influence of our consciousness on the wheel of fortune. Rit involves making a conscious decision in the light of knowledge, and then performing the right action without hesitation. Rit can signify the whole wheel of the year. We must bring our lives into harmony with the ever-wheeling cycles of existence if we are to live a reasonably successful life. Rit represents the channeling of our energies in an appropriate manner in order to produce the desired results. Here, the ritual emphasis is upon being present in the right place at the right time, and performing the appropriate act according to the correct form. In its shape, this rune is formed from the previous one, As, by the addition of a single stroke, making it a sacred enclosure with the connotations of the wheel circling around the periphery to define the interior.

In the Scots dialect, the word *rit* has the meaning of "to score, incise, scratch, or cut"—making an opening or a deliberate mark in something, a new beginning. Physically, it can mean a groove or chasm in rocky ground. The related Scots word, *redd,* means "advice or counsel," but also "a warning, prediction, or foretelling." Rit can be the channeling of energies along a pathway, either physical, as in the case of traveling along a road, or in the case of a rite, where a progression of events takes place in a certain, unvarying, symbolic order. This may also involve physical movement, as in the making of a pilgrimage, or ritual walking along a sacred trackway; known in the

Northern Tradition by its French name of *Yries*. Such ritual walking, often on straight alignments up holy hills, is a recognition and propitiation of the spirit of Mother Earth. Important examples of these exist to this day in various parts of Europe. The ancient pagan sacred sites still exist, because churches were built upon them, and the paths between them survive as tracks, roads, city lanes, and streets. Two of the most important survivors are the north-south alignment of churches that leads to the Lindenhof in Zürich, and in England at a shrine of the wheel-saint, St. Catherine's Hill at Winchester. In Ireland, there is the connected tradition of fairy paths that lead in straight lines from rath to rath (ancient hill-fort earthworks). On certain sacred days of the year, such as Samhain (All Saints' Day, November 1, the Celtic festival of the dead), spirits, fairies, and other inhabitants of the supernatural kingdom march in procession. These supernatural beings were considered to be protectors of the earth, and their path was inviolable, holy ground upon which it was unthinkable to build.

Here, the esoteric meaning of the "journey" is that undertaken by the soul after death, from the burial mound to other worlds. Chariots and other wheeled vehicles were buried with the dead in ancient times. In folk tradition, ritual perambulations of a sacred area were carried out using a wagon on which an image of the deity was placed. This includes the chariot of the sun, carrying the solar disc, and pagan divinities as well as Christian saints.

As a rite, Rit can be interpreted in terms of chivalry and honorable conduct in general, requiring control and initiative in the enforcement of right. In medieval times, the chivalric code of the knight was a spiritual pathway, defending the rights of the individual. Orders such as the Knights Templar were founded with the specific intention of guarding the roads so that pilgrims bound for Jerusalem would be free from attack by bandits. Rit is thus a symbol of pilgrimage. It can signify the archetypal pattern of the universal labyrinth, symbol of the Earth Mother Goddess and the journey of the soul from her at birth and back to her at death. In pagan tradition, Troy was the center of the world, and, in England, an alternative name for the labyrinth is Troy Town. The path to the center of the labyrinth is a similar symbolic centering, where the journey, the path, and the spiritual way are the same thing.

The old English Morris dances and other ceremonial dances that involved movement in a specific way along a specific route are another version of the ritual motion of Rit. On a global scale, the rune Rit indicates the correct path that the earth/human partnership should take. Rit is a rune to be used for healing the earth, restoring it to balance. This is symbolized in this card by the green Stone of the Wise, the shining ball that we call home—our mother planet, the earth.

The equivalent tarot trump to Rit is The Hierophant, a very formalized ritual card, traditionally denoting a guardian of the doctrines and rituals of the faith. The ruling tree of Rit is the wayfaring tree. Rad's corresponding element is air, and the ruling divinities are the earth-fertility deities, Ing and Nerhus. Rit has a male polarity. Its time-cycle position is the half month from August 29 until September 13.

In an upright reading, this card indicates determined movement in particular and determined action in general. It signifies the correct ordering of things, perhaps the way back onto a good course after problems have caused a deviation from one's plans. Rit involves taking control of things, the exercise of leadership. G. Hickes's ancient runic collection, *Linguarum Vett Septentrionalum Thesaurus* (1703-5), translates the rune as having a meaning of "good judgment." Here, it may apply to making a decision between two possibilities, two lovers, two offers of employment, or two proposals of any kind, each of them equally attractive. The querent should trust his or her judgment here, as Rit indicates that the correct route will be chosen. In negotiations, Rit specifies mutual agreement, a situation in which both sides benefit. But it also maintains the rights of the individual in a relationship. Where movement is indicated, Rit can mean that the querent is to go on a journey accompanied by sociable fellow travelers. On a rather shallow level, this card indicates that the querent will receive a message. Spiritually, Rit indicates that seeking outside the normal, seemingly safer, channels of experience is more likely to bring results, so long as fundamental principles are not compromised.

Inverted, the rune denotes disruption of the inquirer's plans. It indicates that one may need to take a journey at an inconvenient time. Perhaps this will come as a sudden, urgent summons to visit someone. But when this call comes, there will be difficulties in travel in the form of delays caused by strikes, bureaucracy, breakdowns, accidents, or simply losing one's way. On a more general level, Rit inverted indicates serious disruption of schemes and projects, a failure for things to work out as they should. Negotiations underway may suddenly come to an end, owing to intransigence on the part of others, unprofessional collaborators, and other influences beyond the questioner's control. Through lack of vigilance, one might be cheated or suffer at the hands of unscrupulous companions. But from a positive point of view, inverted Rit warns us against taking a certain road to ruin and advises us instead to make a new beginning.

KAN

Old German, Kenaz; Gothic, Kusma; Anglo-Saxon, Cenk; Old Norse, Kaun.

The sixth rune is Kan, the rune of the autumnal equinox, ruling the period from September 13 until September 28. The card for Kan depicts an autumnal tree. Symbolically, the trunk points directly upwards, to the region of the gods, while the branch points to the right-hand side, the direction of consciousness. The falling leaves indicate that anything can only exist under appropriate conditions, in harmony with its true nature. A falling leaf can only go downward, from above to below; conversely, an air-bubble in the water can only rise to the surface above from below. But things beyond the confines of direct expense can behave differently, in a transformational manner, as with the sun, which appears to rise and set.

The name of this rune represents the flaming torch, or the internal fire. This can be expressed either in the form of inner illumination (the Old German and Anglo-Saxon meanings), or esoterically as a hot spot, such as an ulcer or swelling (the Gothic and Old Norse readings).

It is the use of controlled fire by human beings. The Old English Rune Poem tells us: "The torch is living fire, bright and shining. Most often, it burns where noble people are at rest indoors." The literal meaning of Kan, then, is the flaming torch that was used in ancient times for illuminating the royal hall. By extension, it also means the resinous pine branches from which torches were made. Symbolically, Kan signifies illumination, brought into being by transformation. The heat and light of the torch come into being through the destruction of the pine wood. Figuratively, Kan brings light to us in the darkness, allowing us to see what is really there, but that had been hidden from our view. Esoterically, the inner light is the bringer of knowledge.

This rune's name, Kan, is cognate with the Celtic word *cen,* which means "powerful." In Cornish *can* means "bright light," while in Scottish dialect *ken* means "knowledge," "one's own mind," "sight of something or recognition." Here, *ken* can also mean "to destroy," in the specific meaning of "burn up." Spiritually, it represents the illumination within the enlightened. But inner illumination is worthless unless it shines forth as a beacon to illuminate others who dwell in darkness. In addition, this torch of knowledge which burns away ignorance must be handed on from generation to generation if it is to have continuity. To that end, Kan brings strength and clarity of thought and the power of concentration within a context of knowledge.

As a means of transformation, fire is the power of the forge where seemingly useless matter is transformed by human will and skill into useful metal. Because transformation brings a new beginning, Kan refers to starting. Another sort of transformation comes with travel, and a variant of the rune is Kano, the name of a small sea-going vessel known as a skiff (Kahn). This type of boat was sacred to the goddess Nertha (Nerthus), being used in her rites around her sacred island of Walcharen. It was also considered to be a ship of the dead, ferrying the soul to "the other side." Kan's other fire aspect is transformation through the funeral pyre, the release of the soul for rebirth in a new body.

Kan signifies one of the two polar principles of existence, the active as contrasted with the passive. Kan is the mystical creation by the union and transmutation of two separate entities of a new third entity. We can only live in a state of balance between the polarities— not by extremes, which have no continuity. Balance is achieved through transformation, and, appropriately, Kan is the rune ruling the time period of the autumnal equinox. Kan is a rune of ability through knowledge which channels protective energy and regenerative powers, and enhances positive actions. It expresses the positive aspects of sexual love imminent in the goddess Freyja and the god Frey. But is in under the overall rulership of Heimdall and the element fire. Being symbolic of the eternal flow of the life-force that is carried and continued through the female of the species, Kan has a female polarity. In the tarot, this rune parallels the trump The Lovers, which signifies the merging together of the opposites in unity.

The rune is usually written as a straight stave, from which emerges a branch. This form reflects the active, generative principle. This is the opposite of Is, the eleventh rune, which is composed of a single stroke which represents the static, neutral principle. Kan is the mystery that tells us that the fire of creation and the fire of destruction are one—the law of the unity of opposites. In the Northern Tradition creation myth, the elements of fire and ice came together in Ginnungagap (space) to create matter. As matter and energy are interchangeable states of existence, matter can be understood poetically as frozen light. As with creation through the interaction of the polarities, Kan signifies the active principle in any partnership. Here, it represents in personal terms the one who is in the position of control. But, to be in control, one must have what is controlled; therefore, even in this condition, the relationship is one of partnership, even if out of balance.

Upright in a runecast, Kan denotes a positive outcome to one's affairs. This may signify success in the querent's struggles against difficulties, which, with appropriate assistance, will be permanent gains. The subject has an active and inquisitive character. The power of successful investigation will enable the querent to gain a hitherto-elusive answer to a certain vexed question. In creative work, this rune is powerful for the artist and craftsperson, indicating work well done. New insights and creative impulses may come into the querent's life, resulting in better work than ever before. Kan's positive attitude foretells that the querent is likely to recover soon from an illness or prolonged bad health. In emotional terms, Kan may signify the potential beginning of a new relationship. In an established relationship, this rune denotes the necessity for learning from one another, gaining personal growth through give and take, and not through dominance. It urges us toward actions appropriate to the condition in which we find ourselves. When combined with other runes of fertility, such as Bar or Ing, Kan may indicate a birth.

Inverted, Kan represents loss of perception and direction. It signifies the involuntary end or voluntary termination of the querent's undertakings. The sudden loss of something important to the subject is indicated. This may be the end of a friendship or emotional relationship such as a marriage, or the loss of knowledge or records, depending on the other runes in the spread. Kan inverted signifies the withdrawal of an offer, or the failure of a project that was just beginning, perhaps the termination of one's employment. Inverted Kan emphasizes delays when cast in conjunction with binding or delaying runes such as Is and Not, or reversed Odal.

GEBO

Old German, Gebo; Gothic, Giba; Anglo-Saxon, Gyfu.

The seventh rune is Gebo (Gyfu), which in all versions signifies a gift or the act of giving. This rune bears the archetypal "lucky number" seven, signifying the gift of good fortune. The card for Gebo depicts a rugged, rocky landscape. In her apparent motion, the sun had "gone behind" a rock, cutting us off from her rays. But now, once more, her beams shine upon us, bringing us the gift of light and energy. As the sun travels westward, to sink beneath the horizon, she gives up our world to the darkness of night. The sun's rule thus gives way in due course to the period ruled by the moon, but again to bring warmth after a time of quiet and humidity.

The gift of Gebo can be seen as the "gift of the gods," which has the more precise meaning of one's own native ability or talent. The possession of a talent morally requires its use in society in a socially responsible manner to be of any lasting value. Therefore, the major meaning of Gebo is unification through the means of exchange. Gebo emphasizes the essential unity between donor and recipient.

This rune's entry in the Old English Rune Poem reads: "To people, giving is a support and ornament of value, and to every outsider without any other, it is substance and honor." The social character of the rune is seen in linking the apparently separate parts of society, and the human race in general with the divine. An interchange between individuals or between people and gods also signifies cooperation between two individuals. This cooperation may be in the form of common cause, a cooperative business venture, or any event that may involve a voluntary sacrifice of one's resources to help others. Giving is not a one-sided act, for the recipient is indebted to the giver by receiving the gift. This is the law of compensation: everything in the universe tends to return to balance. No gift is given in return for nothing; there must be some reflection toward the giver, even if it is only gratitude.

In ancient Northern Europe, the donation of gifts to loyal supporters was a major binding ritual performed by clan chiefs and kings. That donation was an important symbolic function can be seen from the Norse kings, who were titled "givers of rings" after their practice of giving loyalty rings to their earls. These royal gifts were accepted with the full knowledge that the recipients were expected to give their lives in battle fighting for the king if called upon to do so. Specifically, the gift of arms, known as *heriot,* was made to a man on taking service with a war-leader. References to the giving of heriot can be found in many surviving Teutonic and Anglo-Saxon laws and wills. As with the meaning of the rune Gebo, the heriot was a gift which brought obligations. A kenningful poem, written in the early eleventh century by Sigvat to his lord, King Olaf, records such a gift of heriot: "I received thy sword with pleasure, O Njord of Battle, and I have not reviled it since, for it is my joy. This is a glorious way of life, O Tree of Gold; we have both done well. Thou hast gained a good follower, and I a good liege lord."

Here, Gebo is a present, often marking a rite of passage. In the Northern Tradition, Gebo is personified by the Vanir goddess, the

Lady Freja. She was often represented as the goddess Friagabis or under her by-name of Gevn, both of which mean "the bountiful giver." Gebo's elemental correspondence is air; its polarity both female and male, reflecting its linking nature. Its time period in the year cycle comes with the advance of autumn, the season of the second harvest, the harvest of fruit, from September 28 until October 13. The "X" mark of the Gebo rune is used in modern society today as a substitute signature for the illiterate, the mark of a gift, the sigil painted on a tree which is to be cut down (a survival of the mark used to designate the sacrificial object), and the symbol on a letter for a kiss.

Gebo expresses the fundamental law of the unity of opposites, the necessity for two polarities to exist so that dynamism can exert itself between them. Gebo has the secondary meanings of hospitality, generosity, and, in a runecast, may even denote a wedding. Gebo can also refer to agreements between individuals, especially legal contracts. It can express brotherly or sisterly love, or sexual union. In the individual, Gebo signifies the union of the will with actions, that state of balance where one is in harmony with the universal flow of events.

Spiritually, Gebo signifies self-sacrifice for self-awareness. This is the restoration of balance, especially between the mind and body, or between the gods and humanity. Esoterically, this is expressed by the principle of reflection; the rune's mirror image is identical to its original form. This card expresses that image of source and reflection. The white light of the sun is reflected by the moon, its complementary figure. The source, the light, and the reflector form a partnership, and Gebo expresses this system. Because of its compensatory nature, magically, Gebo has been used to deflect harm, acting as a crossing-out of harmful intentions, or as a barrier across the way. Like the later rune Not, Gebo is a rune that links other adjacent runes together, either in a magical working or in a runic divination.

Gebo is the first of the nine non-invertible runes whose meanings are the same whichever way up they are drawn. These runes can have no reversed meaning in the sense that the inverted rune signifies the exact opposite to the upright rune. However, in this card deck, as in certain runestone sets, the direction of the rune can be seen. In general, unlike other runes or tarot cards, inversion does not indicate complete reversal of meaning. An inverted card of a non-invertible rune will indicate a diminished effectiveness, or a reduced strength, of the qualities associated with that rune.

Gebo is one of the most beneficial of runes to appear in a reading. Specifically, the rune signifies the querent's will, and the way that it will be effected in the physical world. It may refer to one's special talents, and the means of using them to their best advantage. Also, it may signify the receipt or giving of a gift, personal generosity, and hospitality given and received. Whatever the question, this rune indicates that there will be a satisfactory result to one's undertakings. It refers especially to a successful partnership or a stable, mutually satisfying emotional relationship. When Gebo appears inverted in a reading, it may indicate the querent giving something away. This could mean making some self-sacrifice for a loved one, or giving up a cherished possession; but equally, the abandonment of outworn ideas or beliefs. Generally, when reversed, this rune has the meaning of the dissolution of barriers, separation, and the breaking of bonds. But because of the beneficial nature of this rune, this dissolution will be advantageous to the querent.

WUNJO

The eighth rune is Wunjo (Wyn), the final rune in the ætt of Frey and Freyja. The card for Wunjo shows a mandrake root in the form of a weathervane. The weathervane turns with the wind, and thus simultaneously both follows and displays the laws of nature. This wind vane stands at the center of things, between the four winds. Thus, Wunjo symbolizes wholeness expressed in terms of encompassing the four directions and the corresponding four winds. The rune's name Wunjo or Wyn is connected with the word "wind," personified by the Celtic god Vintios, whose gusts and gales are irresistible. (In the Norse religion, Odin is the god of the winds.) If we attempt to hold the weathervane in a certain position against the wind, we are acting against nature's logic. Only when we come into harmony with nature can we experience delight, wonder, bliss, and happiness.

In the Old German and Anglo-Saxon languages, this rune signifies the joy that one can achieve by being in a harmonious condition within a largely disharmonious world. The Old English Rune Poem expresses it as: "Joy is for someone who knows little sorrow, without sorrow. He will have bright fruits and happiness and houses enough." The Gothic version of the rune name means "pasture," suggesting carefree summer days and contented, well-fed livestock on the farm—those moments of joy which we should savor in a world which can seem desperately harsh sometimes.

Joy is the condition of the ideal life to which we all aspire. Like all ideals, of course it is unattainable, but nevertheless it is an image to which we must aspire if we are to have hope in our lives. Wunjo is primarily a rune of balance, that mid-point between polar extremes which is necessary to attain so that we can lead a sane and happy existence. Wunjo represents the achievement of one's desires, and the fulfillment of one's will. This happy state can be achieved by bringing one's life into harmony with the prevailing conditions. On a material level, Wunjo signifies the satisfaction to be gained from craftsmanship, the possession of pride and joy in one's work (generally skilled manual work rather than intellectual).

On a spiritual level, Wunjo signifies the transformation of one's life for the better. An important spiritual aspect of Wunjo is attraction, in which individuals are brought into harmony with one another. Wunjo expresses the quality of linking several disparate things or people together in agreement and concord. Wunjo is thus the rune of pluralistic co-existence, symbolizing fellowship, shared aims and the general well-being of the community. The rune is sacred to the deity Vjofn, goddess of reconciliation, whose duty is to incline obstinate people toward love. Secondarily, it is sacred to both Frigg and Odin, and the element air. It is of male polarity, and it covers the half-month from October 13-28, when Hagal's half-month commences.

In the tarot, Wunjo parallels trump 0, The Fool, a being outside the bounds of good and evil whose will is in harmony with the flow of events. The Fool represents light without shadow, and in the Wunjo card, he is shown in the shadow of yellow light. Holding a magic wand in his right hand, he rises up toward the highest place. He symbolizes the power of the will which has risen to the highest point. Beneath him is the labyrinth, the troublesome path, the means of attaining the objective only after many detours. But joy is often the result of much trouble. In this way, the rune has a link with Rit, the pathway itself. Beneath the mandrake, the earth is carpeted with blooming flax, the color of the yellow light which envelopes the rune itself. To the left is the hazy shape of a dolphin or whale, informing us that it is still possible for us to discover hidden possibilities of communication—and to learn from them.

When Wunjo falls upright in a runic divination, the rune presages an excellent outcome in everything the querent wants to know about. One will be fortunate in all matters, potentially with a transformation of one's life toward better things. Wunjo indicates removal of any alienation that one may experience in society, as well as integration and harmonious dealings with all people. More specifically, Wunjo can indicate the imminent receipt of good news. Any plans for travel will be successfully accomplished in the most pleasant way possible. Emotional links should be successful and joyful, and any joint ventures will bind the querent and his or her partners together in harmonious fellowship. Spiritually, Wunjo indicates joyful spiritual experiences in concord with others.

Inverted, Wunjo indicates the opposite of joy, unhappiness, misery, and personal ruin. The subject's will is weak and thwarted. Imbalances of all kinds are likely to be felt, with multiple problems impinging upon one another to create a chaotic, hectic life where there can be no peace of mind. At work, the reversed rune designates unhappiness, dissatisfaction with unpleasant conditions, drudgery, delay, obstructive superiors, unyielding bureaucracy, and petty disruptions of all kinds. Rivals and opponents may use underhanded methods to destroy the querent's prospects. When connected with travel, Wunjo inverted denotes unpleasant and uncomfortable conditions, troublesome petty officialdom, and perhaps not even arriving at one's destination at all. In a relationship, it signifies disappointment in love, underhanded actions by one's partner, problems with third parties, or perhaps even deliberate agitation by troublemakers. The indicated result is loss of affection. Spiritually, it indicates turmoil and uncertainty. Overall, when Wunjo is inverted, it indicates to the inquirer that there is an urgent necessity for caution in decisions, and that he or she should not make any decisions at this time.

ḢAGAL

Old German, Hagalaz; Gothic, Hagl; Anglo-Saxon, Haegl; Old Norse, Hagall.

Hagal is the first rune of the second ætt of eight runes. This makes it rune number nine, the most sacred number of Northern Tradition spirituality. Nine is the number of completion and wholeness, symbolizing the universe, the nine worlds of Yggdrassil, "the power of three times three."

Hermann Haindl's card for Hagal depicts the rune in the form of a cosmic mandrake root—the Hag-alraune. The roots of this mystic mandrake symbolize the six directions of space. At the center-point of the roots is a hexagonal crystal representing the central source of all existence. Here, Hagal is like the roots of the cosmic tree, Yggdrassil, among which, according to legend, dwarves and elves live, work, and play. The elves or fairies, which represent spirituality, are winged; while the dwarves of the earth, which represent the heavy, material world, do not possess wings. Likewise, the bird and serpent symbolize upper and lower natures, brought together by the formative forces inherent in Hagal.

In the present version of the Elder Futhark used in divination, there are two forms of the Hagal rune. The first is shaped like something between the Roman letters "N" and "H," and the second is the six-branched form used in this card deck. The former shape is the earlier form of the stave, but the six-branched one more appropriately represents the esoteric qualities inherent in the rune. In all versions of its name, Hagal has the literal meaning of "hail," expressed here in the Old English Rune Poem:

—⚡—

"Hail is the whitest of grains.
It sweeps from the sky,
Whirled by the blowing wind,
It then turns to water."

—⚡—

Through the image of hail, which is the icy crystallization of rain through cold, the rune Hagal represents the primal seed of manifestation and transformation. Soon after the falling hail reaches the ground, the solid hailstones become liquid. After doing its damage, the potentially life-threatening hailstone is transformed almost magically into benevolent and life-supporting water.

This runic stave is often known as the "mother rune" because it is a basic geometric form from which the shapes of the other runes can be generated. More importantly, it is the mother rune because it symbolizes formative causation, the underlying structural matrix of the physical universe. Although this is a vastly complex pattern which is usually invisible and beyond conscious understanding, it is the fundamental structure without which there could be no existence. The fundamental nature of this Hagal pattern can be seen in the basic geometric structure of matter, the hexagonal lattice. This form is found in nature as the basic arrangement of molecular and crystalline structures. The formation of natural patterns conform to the arrangement we call Hagal: cracks in the ground, ice and quartz crystals, bone formation in animals, and the cellular structure of plants. Through their intuition, the ancient runemasters recognized the nature of this pattern many centuries before the invention of the microscope established it scientifically. This is a powerful demonstration of the inner access to the primal qualities of the universe which the runes can provide.

Geometrically, the Hagal pattern is the fundamental form. It can be drawn as the basic six-fold division of the circle, as the circle's radius is exactly one-sixth of its circumference. Much of classical geometry stems from this basic perception. Following the rune Wunjo, which can represent the four directions of north, east, south, and west, as the ninth rune, Hagal adds another dimension: above and below, sky and earth. On the physical level, the Hagal rune signifies the six directions of space: forward and backward; left and right; up and down. It signifies the three axes of space, the mathematical coordinates x, y, and z. These are the roots of matter. The Hagal rune also depicts the geometry of the cube when seen from one corner. In esoteric terms, this is the mystic cube of light, manifested in Hagal as the six parallel lines radiating from the center. These six outward points represent the cosmos, and the seventh, the central point, is a mystic representation of the divine source. Behind this central location is the obscured eighth point, the unseen but ever-present solar power. This card shows this sacred point in the form of a crystal with a hexagonal vertex. As a container of the divine spark, Hagal's name is cognate with words for "holy" and "complete," the English "whole," the German *heilig,* etc.

As the mother rune, the center of all things, Hagal represents the access point to other dimensions or states of consciousness. It is the psychic entry point to the cosmic axis, which links the upper world with the middle and lower worlds. In geomancy, this point is knows as the Omphalos, Umbilicus, or Nowl, the navel of the world, often manifested in physical form as a crossroads marked by a standing stone or cross.

The six-branched form of Hagal mirrors the eternal mystery of the microcosm and the macrocosm, in which the greater world (the universe) is reflected in the lesser world (the human being). In this card deck, the Hagal rune is shown here as being composed of alrauns or *erdmannekins,* the central European equivalent of the mandrake. Alrauns were the roots of certain plants, such as the bryony, carved into human form. They were believed to be inhabited by earth spirits, sacred to the goddess of the crossroads. Alrauns were helpers during childbirth. They also brought rejuvenation to the old, provided protection against bad weather, and, when laid on the bed, could prevent nightmares. The runes carved on an alraun were known as *hellrunes,* after Hela, the Hag-goddess of the underworld, who is one aspect of the Goddess of the Crossroads. As the rune of Hela, the Hagal rune can manifest itself as the Hag-alraun. Its tree is the yew, a sacred stock customarily associated with the dead and still planted in cemeteries to this day. In the runic year circle, Hagal is the rune ruling the time period containing the old Celtic festival of the dead, Samhain, celebrated after dark on October 31 in Great Britain and the United States as Halloween. (The runic period covered by Hagal runs from October 28 until November 13.)

Another connection between this rune and the cosmic axis is its association with the world serpent, which, in Norse cosmology, coils around the base of the World Tree yggdrassil. This serpent, Nidhöggr, continuously gnaws away at the tree, threatening its stability. Symbolically, the serpent is the threat to stability inherent in all stable systems. The potential sudden catastrophic change inherent in the rune Hagal from its static crystalline form to its flowing, liquid form. This image of the serpent and Hagal is alluded to in the Old Icelandic Rune Poem, which states: "Hagal is a cold seed, a sleet-fall, and a plague of snakes."

In this aspect, the rune is a northern parallel of the serpent-bearing stave, or caduceus, of the Roman deity Mercury, god of flow and transformation. Hagal is that pattern of energy which, originating in the past, is active in the present time, with a powerful if subtle influence. Accordingly, it is the power of evolution within the framework of present existence. Hagal is the rune at the roots of things, both on a physical, material level and in time. Hagal's ætt is ruled over by Heimdall, the watcher of the gods, guardian of the entrance to the upperworld; and Mordgud, guardian goddess of the entrance to the underworld. Under his by-name, Rig, "The Agitator," Heimdall was traditionally the organizer of the classes of agrarian-hunting society. Rig is also associated with the rune Rit, and generally "setting things straight." But, spiritually, Hagal is ruled by the oldest Norn, Urd, who weaves the Web of Wyrd. The Nornic woven threads symbolize those events, which, though in the past, still have an influence upon us. This concept is best known as karma. In the Northern Tradition, it is known as our Wyrd, the result of events in our past life, and the lives of others with whom we have interacted, which influence and construct our present lives.

Preeminently in the runes, Hagal is the symbol of the personal unconscious mind and of the formative process of thought. In more specific terms, it can be thought of as a disruptive or admonishing agency which works in our unconscious to bring much-needed change and ultimately make us alter some of our more cherished ideas. It can also indicate unavoidable changes in our life's course. At the final account, this disruptive agency has an internal origin, in our own past. It can be the final result of unsolved problems, unresolved conflicts, and unlearned lessons. Hagal shows us that now is the time to deal with these problems if we are to progress further. Once we have recognized this necessity, we are empowered to do something meaningful.

Hagal is the ruler of the runes known as *hogrunes* or *hugrunes,* the runes of the mind, meditation upon which can bring one to a state of mental clarity. They are symbolized by one of Odin's ravens, Huginn (thought) and Hagal's own color correspondence, light blue.

Consciousness of our own position, however bad things may be, gives us the means of dealing with the problem. So the form of the rune Hagal is a protective sigil, known as the lucky star, which is drawn geometrically with a pair of compasses as arcs within a circle. It can be seen painted or carved on many old buildings in places as far and wide as Germany, England, and Pennsylvania, still serving its protective function against bad weather and the entrance of disharmony into the household. The element of Hagal is the Northern Tradition's fifth element, ice.

Hagal is one of the nine non-invertible runes in the Elder Futhark; the shape of Hagal remains the same whichever way up it falls. This unchanging shape symbolizes the eternal cosmic harmony and our unavoidable position in the world—our örlog, and from it, our own personal "fate"—our Wyrd. There is no way that we can avoid our Wyrd. It is inevitable, whichever way we look at it. But once the runes have given us some insight into our Wyrd, we have a real choice whether to ignore the warnings or to act on them. However we act, we make a conscious decision stemming from our own free will. The key to Hagal in a divination is that interaction between those events over which we have no control, and our own free will to deal with them.

Many rune readers have traditionally given Hagal a bad significance, heralding a disruption in the querent's life. Such a disruption may take place as the result of accidents, "acts of God," and generally unforeseen bad luck. The events presaged by Hagal may arrive suddenly, without warning, outside and beyond the control of the querent; but they will proceed according to already established rules, such as in a court of law. Furthermore, the outcome of the event will be impersonal and inexorable, and have nothing to do with human emotions or preferences. Here, Hagal signifies an extra-human process rather than the results of human action. However bad an outcome may be indicated, there is nothing personal in it. When human agency is involved, it will be through the medium of large organizations, bureaucracy, and legal processes. Here, Hagal can indicate the receipt of news or information, perhaps via a letter. Hagal teaches us that the best way of coping with life is to come as closely as possible into harmony with nature, both with the natural cycles of the seasons and with our own true nature. Then, whatever happens to us, the means to deal with it is present within our own free will. If we follow the traditional teaching "know thyself," then we will be able to live creatively within our own Wyrd, in harmony with our own natures and with the environment in which we live.

NOT

Old German, Naudhiz; Gothic, Nauths; Anglo-Saxon, Nyd; Old Norse, Naud.

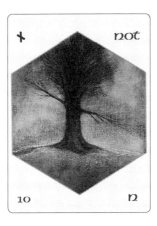

The tenth rune is Not, also known as Nyd. Hermann Haindl's painting for the rune card shows a beech tree standing alone on a hill in a frosty winter landscape. It is just after sunset, and the tree appears as a barrier, blocking the way forward. Like arms, two branches stand out from the main trunk of the tree. On the left side of the picture, the branch points upward; on the right side, it points downward. It resembles a Sufic "dervish" dancer, who takes the energies of the earth with one arm, and the energies of the sky with the other; or a pair of scales, weighed down on one side. This form can be interpreted as the "scales of justice" or the "balance of necessity." With Not, it is the conscious side which is too heavy. We need balance and justice. Symbolically, this is the "law-tree" or "tree of measure" of the Eddas.

The Gothic meaning of this rune is "necessity," while in Old German and Anglo-Saxon, this rune literally signifies need. The Old Norse meaning is "distress" or "constraint." Not may be interpreted as the kind of need that stems from the absence or scarcity of some-thing. This sort of need is described in the Old English Rune Poem: "Need is a tight band across the chest, but often it can be transformed into a bringer of help, if attended to early." As well as describing need, or more precisely, necessity, the Anglo-Saxon rune poet's words also incorporate a more philosophical concept: the power to be released from need can be found within the need itself.

In the rune-row, Not comes between Hagal and Is, hail and ice respectively. Here, Not is the frost on the ground between the hail and the ice. In the runic time circle, all three runes come at the time of year when winter is taking hold. Hagal rules the period from October 28 until November 13; Not from November 13 until November 28; and Is from November 28 until December 13. These three runes denote a time of year when action is limited, and one must act carefully at all times.

Caution in one's actions is called for by Not, and, as with the pre-vious rune, the philosophical maxim "know thyself" is particularly applicable here. This can be interpreted practically as not trying to strive against our Wyrd, but instead, understanding it and using it constructively. Not is the rune of that semimythical place, Thule, whose name translates as "that place where one is forced to turn back." Constraint tells us, "this far, and no further." Not is also a rune of magical protection, used in former times as Ale-rune to protect drinking vessels and the drink they held against contamination, both physical and magical.

In the Northern Tradition legend, the goddess of night was called Nott. She had three husbands, by all of whom she bore children. By the first husband, Naglfari, she bore a son, Aud; by the second husband, Annar, a daughter, Jörd, the earth goddess; and by her third husband, Dellinger, a son, Dag (day). Thus the goddess of the rune Not (Nott) is the mother of the twenty-fourth rune, Dag. This concept is present in the traditional reckoning of days beginning with sunset. Thus the Northern Tradition festival of Beltane (May Day,

May 1) begins at sunset on April 30. Similarly, all ancient traditional festivals begin with an "eve," the dark period out of which comes the light of morning. Symbolically, in this aspect of its meaning, the shape of the Not rune imitates the fire-bow and block which was used customarily to ignite the needfire. In this way, like the goddess Nott, mother of day, the fire-bow and block of Not is the mother of firelight.

Naturally, the element of Not is fire. Its ruling deities are the goddess Nott and Skuld, the Norn of "that which is to come." In this aspect, Not signifies that balance to which all things must return in the long run, and, consequently, justice. As justice, Not's shape echoes balance, the attribute of the Northern justice-goddess Var, punisher of oath-breakers.

Traditionally, Not is the third of the nine non-invertible runes, which makes its interpretation equally restrictive whatever way up it falls. But in some representations, it is possible to tell which is upright and which is inverted. This card set has that possibility. But whichever way up Not occurs in a runecast, a fairly negative outcome is indicated. Either way, the querent should feel warned to examine his or her plans before making any decision to continue with them. Upright, Not signifies limitations of all kinds, but not necessarily insuperable limitations. In a runecast, Not may denote a shortage or scarcity of something that the querent needs. This is less likely to be a lack of money than an absence of material to work with, "writers' block," or the drying-up of artistic creativity. In combination with other runes, this scarcity may be defined more precisely as lack of partnership or co-workers, lack of funds, or, potentially more disastrous, as working in the wrong environment. This blockage can only be overcome by patiently working toward one's objective, even when the odds seem to be against one.

Not may refer to long-standing illnesses or disablement which prevents one from achieving their goals, but also indicates that one should strive to bypass or otherwise overcome these handicaps. The achievement of justice designated by this rune can be achieved only by patient striving against the odds. But only when Not falls with other negative runes is the meaning of the rune to be taken as failure or total loss. One shouldn't see a Not rune as specifying abandonment of one's projects or relationships. Upright, in conjunction with other, more success-oriented runes, such as Feo, As, or Sig, it may be taken as a warning against making any previously-planned changes. One is urged to keep the status quo.

Inverted, Not denotes something amiss that causes an impediment to the free flow of events. Inappropriate conditions are prevalent, with the inevitability of failure if the present course is maintained. Perhaps the inquirer is attempting to use incorrect or inappropriate responses to a problem, acting against their own or others' better judgment. These problems and constraints on action may be the consequences of one's örlog, seen personally as the revenge of the past on the present. There must be reparation for one's past mistakes, perhaps in the form of hardship or even punishment. Here, justice is to the querent's disadvantage, but is necessary spiritually that it should happen for balance to be regained. Although there could be the possibility of immediate gains, these may be achieved by unethical means. In any case, these gains will not be maintained, and it is likely that failure will be the ultimate result.

IS

Old German, Isa; Anglo-Saxon, Is; Old Norse, Iss.

The eleventh rune is Is (Isa); literally, "ice." This rune symbolizes the principle of static existence. The rune card depicts a column of ice rising to the heights from a fog-shrouded, wintry mountainscape. It is isolated and alienated from its surroundings, rising so high above Mother Earth that it loses contact with her. All around is a bleak vision of icy coldness, illuminated by a faint pink glow, the last rays of the weak winter sun. There is a strong separation of the light and the dark parts of the column. But the light comes from the right, the side of consciousness. The I-consciousness rises straight up, immobile, frozen, petrified. It is irresistible because it is immovable.

The form of the rune symbolizes the icicle, or the frozen waterfall on the cliffside. It is also the form of the straight sword-blade, "the Ice of Battle," of the Old Norse kenning. The Old English Rune Poem says: "Ice is very cold and slippery. It shines like glass, jewel-like. A frost-covered field is a fair sight."

Ice is formed when water loses heat energy. By losing energy, water also loses it fluidity and takes on a hard, resistant quality, quite different from its former condition. The frozen earth, glittering with frost, signifies awesome barrenness. The only wealth is the aesthetic beauty of the jewel-like ice crystals, which is not something which can be used practically by human beings. Is represents the principle of inertia, the polar opposite of the rune Kan. But at the temperature range present on this planet, ice always has the potential of melting, becoming fluid once more.

Although ice is crystalline and cannot flow like water, it can move *en masse*. When it does move, it does so as a glacier, exceedingly slowly; but nevertheless it exercises an irresistible force. The other way ice can move is by floating in the ocean as an iceberg, where Is deceptively shows only one-ninth of its true bulk above the surface. In Northern mythology, this cold, inexorable power is symbolized by the Ice Giants and the goddess Rinda, the personification of the hard and frozen earth.

The time period of the year covered by the rune Is extends from the end of November and the early part of December, when the cold winter has taken its grip upon the northern world (November 28 to December 13). Is prevents growth; it is the counter-force to evolution, both material and spiritual. Is has the power to keep things as they are, whether for good or for ill. This rune's polarity is female, and its element is ice. It is under the rulership of the middle Norn, Verdandi, "that which is eternally becoming."

On a more symbolic level, the rune Is represents the elongated crystals of quartz used by shamans throughout the world as receptacles of sacred power. Many sorts of crystal, but especially those of quartz, are magical instruments of continuity in the shamanic tradition. In traditional societies, a quartz crystal would be inserted into an incision in the shaman's body, which then was sewn up. The crystal remained in the body for the duration of the shaman's life. When the shaman died, the crystal was removed from his remains and passed on to his or her successor, to be sewn inside his or her body. In this way, the life experience of the shamanic continuity was maintained and added to by the successive lives of those who carried the crystal. Magically, or physically, the experiences of the shamans were record-ed within the crystal as a resource to be drawn upon as needed.

Is is the fourth of the nine non-invertible runes, where its mean-ing is the same when upside-down. In a reading, Is indicates that there is a major obstacle in the way of progress, and represents some of the more damaging, uncontrollable, suppressive aspects of the world around us. Is denotes stillness and inertia, the cessation of progress, or the termination of a relationship due to powerful, inex-orable forces beyond the querent's control. Here, it acts as "the ice of battle," terminating things in the same way that a sword terminates lives. Is denotes that one may be frustrated in all attempts at chang-ing things, leading to the vicious circle of failure and frustration, with a consequent loss of dynamism. When Is appears in a divination, it specifies that, at present, there is no possibility of a change in cir-cumstances. Projects underway are likely to slow down and be delayed in their implementation. This suggests that the projects in question should be frozen for the time being. In a relationship, Is signifies the cooling down of emotions, a loss of warmth between partners, distancing, and perhaps separation through indifference on both sides. Disagreements with relatives or friends are also indicated. In a "worst case" scenario—that is, when the card appeared reversed—Is denotes that drive, energy, and enthusiasm have been frozen out of an undertaking. The inference, in this case, is that the inquirer should give up and start again with a new project or relationship.

JERA

Old German, Jera; Gothic, Jer; Anglo-Saxon, Ger; Old Norse, Ar.

The twelfth rune, and the mid-point on the runic circle, is Jera. The rune card depicts the dynamic rotation of the seasons around the cosmic axis. It signifies the totality of a whole year, the four seasons that are only possible if the heavens and earth cooperate appropriately. A fertile land lies between high mountains and deep lakes. We find our sphere of existence in the middle point between west, north, east, and south. Thus we are part of the present. Each of the four seasons is depicted as forming part of a four-sided garland encircling the upright axis. To the left, the unconscious side, are the seasons of winter and spring, while to the right, the conscious side, are summer and autumn. The axis marks the transition between the winter and the summer halves of the year: at the top, the festival of Beltane (May Day); and at the bottom, the festival of Samhain (November 1). This axis is the transition point between the lower and upper worlds, changing in color from brown to green to blue to signify this connection. The clouds circle around it.

In all its variants, Jera has the meaning of "season" or "year," in the sense of completion. It expresses the eternally cyclic nature of time; Jera signifies the completion of a cycle of any length, most usually the annual cycle. Here, the image is of the rune signifying the coming together of the four seasons of spring, summer, autumn, and winter. In the runic year circle, this rune marks the low point of midwinter/midnight, the time at which the cycle can be seen to both end and begin anew. Jera thus manifests physically that which is imminent within Hagal. Jera represents the successful harvest achieved by appropriate management within the constraints of natural law. If actions are carried out in harmony with the natural order, according to natural law, then the results will be beneficial to all, bringing "abundance for both rich and poor," as it says in the Old English Rune Poem.

As the rune of midwinter, Jera's form expresses its function, facing back to the old year just passed, and forward to the new one just beginning. Its form combines the upright stave of Is, the static force, with the small, involutional version of the Ing rune, the generative force. It is also a back-to-back combination of two Dorn runes. Thus it is supremely protective, both in the conscious and subconscious realms. Overall, its combinational nature reflects the mystic marriage between earth and the cosmos, partners in the cyclic pattern of existence. As a rune of union, Jera is of both male and female polarities, and is thus sacred to the Lord and Lady of the Old Religion, the goddess Freyja and the god Frey. Traditionally, Frey's Norse prayer is the invocation of this rune *Til árs ok fridhar*— "for good season and harvest." Its herb is the aromatic plant rosemary, and its corresponding element is earth.

Jera signifies the twelve- and 24-fold division of the year. This is expressed as the twelve solar months, the twelve signs of the zodiac, the 24 hours in the day and the 24 runic half-months in the year. Jera denotes the cyclical nature of existence, the annual path of the planet earth around the sun, and the rotation of the galaxy on a much larger dimension and a much longer time scale. Although it falls in the midwinter period, it represents the joyous abundance of the midwinter festival of Yule (Christmas), the darkest period of the year when the produce of the harvest is enjoyed to celebrate the beginning of the return of the light. Jera here is the abundant fourth quarter of three non-productive quarters of the year, signified by the preceding three runes, Hagal, Not, and Is. As the twelfth rune, Jera displays the complementary opposite quality of the 24th rune, Dag, signifying involution rather than evolution; return rather than giving out.

Like the previous three runes of Hagal's ætt, Jera is another tra ditionally non-invertible rune, the fifth of nine; here the inversion indicates a less strong manifestation of the reading. Jera is a beneficial rune, promising abundance to all if the correct ways of doing things are followed. Upright in a reading, it indicates that the querent will experience a change for the better, perhaps in the form of abundant return as the result of a past action. It indicates success in business, a good return on an investment, or good payment for work done in the past, such as royalties. Jera can also indicate matters connected with the law: recompense or damages owed the querent, the collecting of dues, or receipt of payments which are due to the querent. To whichever area the question refers, this rune signifies orderliness and good judgment, the gathering of experience and its use in a beneficial way. Jera signifies the reaping of the benefits of long study or having followed an arduous spiritual path. It signifies that the subject is entering a more positive phase in life. Spiritually, this rune marks the end of a dark period of the soul, and a sudden realization that one has achieved awareness.

Inverted, the rune Jera indicates that things will not be as good as they seemed at first. But this is not a negative indication that expresses failure. It shows that things can only happen at the appropriate time, when they are ready, in their proper season. One cannot hurry matters; one must be patient. The querent is warned not to judge others, nor to demand payment from others without first ascertaining their circumstances. As a rune of time, Jera can be used magically to speed up or slow down a process. In a card reading, inclination to the right indicates a speeding-up of the process, while a left-hand inclination denotes that although events seem to be running away rapidly out of control, they will slow down and be brought back into some semblance of order before long.

eoh

Old German, Eihwaz; Gothic, Ailus; Anglo-Saxon, Eoh; Old Norse, Ihwar.

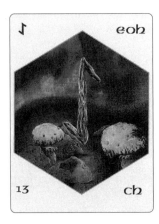

The thirteenth rune is Eoh. The card depicting this rune speaks of above and below; of sky and earth. Its drawn form, a triad of strokes, signifies the union of body, soul, and spirit. The transition between the lower and upper landscape starts below to the left, passing through a rippling motion toward the upper right in a flowing transition. On the ground, there are stones and seemingly poisonous mushrooms. This signifies the reality that to walk on earth is to be constantly in peril. Only the proper, correctly balanced means of using nature is permissible to us, for overuse can lead—and has led—to harm. The form within the rune (depicted, like Hagal, as an alraun) shows that the passage from below to above involves suffering. The "tear" of blood at the vertical central point of the rune symbolizes the suffering which is an integral part of life, the mystery of the "bleeding yew." But remember that tears may be occasioned by both joy and pain.

In all of its linguistic versions, the rune's name represents the yew tree. In the Old English Rune Poem, it is described thus: "On the outside, the yew is a rough tree, hard and fast in the Earth, guardian of the fire, a joy to the home." Of trees native to the north of Europe, the yew lives the longest, sometimes for over a thousand years. In England, some of the most ancient churchyard yew trees are said to be older than the early medieval church that they accompany. They were present as young trees when the sacred place was a pagan sanctuary, before being taken over by the Christian faith. Really ancient trees, which are hollow, having almost lost their hold on life, are often regenerated by their own daughters growing inside them. And exceptional yew trees, where the reddish resin issues incessantly like blood from an unhealed wound, are known as "bleeding yews." In folk tradition, they are held to be especially sacred, even for a holy tree; the spirits of these bleeding yews were the objects of worship. At times of festivity, the trees, which often had their own names, were decked with garlands and ribbons. Having such exceptional characteristics, the yew tree is considered to be the sacred tree of death and rebirth, thus the symbolic function of planting yews in churchyards and cemeteries. The old German adage, which says "Before the yews, no magic can remain," refers to the magically-cleansing attribute of this powerful talismanic tree.

In traditional handicrafts, the wood of the yew tree is recognized as one of the hardest and the most durable. As a local saying from the New Forest in the south of England states, "A post made of yew will outlast a post of iron." The wood of this tree is best known for its use in bow-making. The bow brings death both to animals in hunting and to humans in warfare. To carry a bow in the days before the invention of firearms was a defensive act. Potential assailants could see the formidable weapon and back off. This is one of the defensive qualities of Eoh.

The Norse god of the bow and skis, both of which were made of yew, was Ullr, or Ulli, son of the goddess Sif. In Anglo-Saxon

England, he was worshipped as Vulder, and in parts of Germany, he was Holler, husband of the goddess Holda. Whatever his name, Ullr is a god of hunting and death, more specifically connected with the Wild Hunt, a supernatural band which rode through the countryside at night, taking away wrongdoers. Ullr is a winter god of protection known as "the shield god" both from his shield-shaped snow shoes and from his yew magic. In the Christian tradition, his equivalent is Saint Hubert, who took over some of the god's attributes, as well as Ullr's holy day, November 22. (The actual half-month of the year ruled by Eoh is December 28 until January 13.)

The ancient Irish cultivator and craftsman of the yew, Finntann, is reported to have related to the Árd Righ (High King) of Ireland at Tara the tradition that the first household vessels ever made were fashioned from the wood of the yew tree. As if to affirm this, buckets made of yew have been found as grave goods in Anglo-Saxon burials in England at Linton, Cambridgeshire and at Roundway Down, Wiltshire. They are thought to have a protective function, perhaps containing sacred liquids such as ale. More specifically, Eoh signifies protection as afforded by a yew magic such as that practiced by ancient Northern European shamans. Traditionally, the yew tree and its wood have a number of magical functions. In the graveyard, the yew protected the dead from evil spirits and the ministrations of necromancers. Shamans used the yew for gaining access to the other-world through potentially very dangerous, even life-threatening practices involving the tree's leaves and resin. Magic staves made of the yew were carried as talismans by warriors and seafarers. Runic-inscribed yew staves were rubbed against the body as a magic protection by a warrior about to go into battle, to enhance physical strength. The fiery cross carried by Scottish clansmen to summon their comrades in time of war was made from boughs taken from the yew tree. Similarly, in ancient Holland, a sword made from fire-scorched yew wood was brought from settlement to settlement to summon the warriors to battle.

The poisonous substances present in the yew have also made the tree and its rune one of death. It is no coincidence that Eoh is the traditionally unlucky number thirteen in the rune row, equivalent to the thirteenth card in the tarot, Death. The medieval Bembo Tarot deck shows a skeleton with a bow, reinforcing this link. In northern Scotland, it was believed that a yew branch taken from a graveyard would enable one chief to denounce another in such a way that, although his comrades could hear the threat, the intended victim could hear nothing. There is an Irish legend that one can use a druidic staff of yew, upon which are written the magic formulas known as Powerful Oghams, in order to safely penetrate the fairy kingdom (i.e., the otherworld). Rune tradition sees this as indicating that we should not fear death, for as Eoh, the yew represents the passage of the soul from one state to another.

When writing this rune, first you stroke the pen down, then vertically upwards, and finally, at the top, down a little once more, signifying the link between the triad of body, soul, and spirit. The form of the rune Eoh echoes the traditional magic rune staves made of yew, several Frisian examples of which still survive from as early as the sixth century of the present calendar. The most notable of these are the Britsum stave, dating from the sixth century, and the yew wand from Westeremden, dated around the year 800. These bear appropriate protective inscriptions in runes. The Britsum inscription reads: "Always carry this yew in the battle throng." Yew wood was used to make these sacred objects in order to create powerful magical talismans used in banishing all harm, more specifically the powers of destruction and death. The form of the rune is sometimes known as "the wolf's tooth," a symbol of the grappling-irons used by medieval warriors for scaling walls of besieged towns, or in naval warfare. This emphasizes one of the rune's meanings of communication and connection, more specifically, gaining access. In medieval Germany, the sigil of the Westphalian Vehmgericht was composed of four Eoh runes superimposed upon one another, representing the ever-presence of the court's agents, and hence the ubiquity of their version of law and order throughout the eight directions of space. In its power, then, the yew and the Eoh rune are affirmative of continuity and endurance through all destructive conditions, including inclement weather, war, and even one's own death. In its polarity, Eoh is considered to be a male rune, ruling all five elements (earth, water, ice, air, and fire).

Eoh is the sixth of the nine non-invertible runes. Although magically, Eoh was often called the "death rune," in a runecast it does not mean that the querent is soon to die. The upright card is a good indication. The querent will be successful in his or her endeavors, like an expert archer hitting the target. Eoh denotes the querent's excellent judgment. It is a good sign in seemingly unfavorable circumstances. Events will turn in the querent's favor, perhaps with the assistance of an old acquaintance. When this card is inverted, it indicates that there may be some hindrance or dispute in events which causes minor delay, but in the long term will prove beneficial. There is also the possibility that old problems, which the querent thinks are past, may recur. But when this card appears inverted with an inverted Yr (the 25th rune), then the aspects are very bad indeed. It is probably best not to continue with the rune reading, and to abandon it at that point. The principle of scrapping a reading is well-known in divinatory geomancy, where the rubric at a certain point automatically leads to the abandonment of a reading. When this bad omen appears, no further rune readings should be attempted until the following day.

peorth

Old German, Perthro; Gothic, Paírthra; Anglo-Saxon, Peorð.

The fourteenth rune is Peorth. The rune card portrays the stave with overtones of secrecy and mysticism. It is a chilly, moonlit night. The tree symbolizing the Peorth rune is bent over like a seated human figure viewed from the side, her upper arm seeming to cradle the moon, while the lower arm arches over a hole in the earth, perhaps the entrance to the underworld. Above, the tree's branches grow like flames into the upper air, while the roots spread deeply and firmly into the earth. Thus, Peorth is a rune both of darkness and of light, the one seen as the compliment of the other. The noted Dutch rune-mistress Freya Aswynn has suggested that the Peorth rune can symbolize the womb of the Great Goddess, the Allmother. In this aspect, Peorth signifies the lunar and chthonic aspects of birth. The flower is the aconite, known in Norse folk tradition as Tyr's Helm (the helmet of the Tyr). This poisonous herb stands guard over the unspoken mysteries of life and death.

The meaning of this rune has caused more debate than any of the runes. It has been suggested that in Old German and Gothic, the name refers to a dice cup, a complex medieval randomizing mechanism used for casting lots. A connected meaning, which is believed to be the Anglo-Saxon interpretation, is that Peorth is a chess pawn or game piece, whose movements upon the gameboard symbolize the "ups and downs" of human life. The interpretation of the Peorth rune as a playing piece in a board game symbolizes the dynamic interaction between conscious free will and the constraints of the conditions in which that will must be exercised. The pattern of the gameboard and the rules of the game, the örlog, are already in existence. To play the game at all, the movement of the game pieces must be carried out within this framework. These structural limitations of a game are analogous to life itself, where, through our Wyrd, we are situated. But, just as the actual movements made by the players in any board game are not fixed—being the result of the players' conscious skill— in life, too, we have free will within the constraints of our own Wyrd. Runic divinations can enable us to discover this Wyrd, which otherwise is hidden from us.

The rune Peorth's reference in the Old English Rune Poem is, "A lively tune means laughter and play where brave people sit together in the hall, warriors together, drinking ale." Connected with this "lively tune" is the "lively step"—the dance of life, another meaning ascribed to Peorth. All elements, of the interplay of life, the dance of life, and the gamble that is living, are present here in the rune's meaning.

In the runic year cycle, Peorth's half-month is late January, when the days are becoming appreciably longer once more after the dark days of midwinter. However, there is a traditional English adage, "As the days grow longer, the cold grows stronger," and this applies especially to the half-month of Peorth (January 13 to January 28). The element associated with Peorth is water, and it is sacred to Frigg, who in this case appears in her aspect as the goddess Fortuna. In England, fortune is known as "Lady Luck," to whom all gamblers address their prayers. In the tarot, this rune is connected with trump XXI, The World. Peorth is the paradox of that which is ever-changing, yet ever the same. The shape and meaning of the rune Peorth is functionally the same as the character Peith in the Ogham tree alphabet of the Celts. Peith signifies the snowball tree or guelder rose. The meaning of the Ogham stave is almost identical with that of the rune, underlining the basic unity of the Celtic and the Germanic spiritual traditions. Whichever way we interpret the actual meaning of the rune's name, Peorth is a bringer into being, expressing that which formerly was not apparent. In each interpretation, Peorth brings forth the inherent patterns that underlie the present situation into manifestation. However, this concept does not infer any sort of pre-destination, a belief which has no place in the Northern Tradition.

An upright Peorth card indicates hidden knowledge leading to beneficial secrets coming to light. An inner secret is expressed as the ability to distinguish value from worthlessness. The querent is likely to do well in games of chance and gambling, for he or she possesses the fortuitous ability to guess correctly. Peorth refers also to a secret that the querent wants to remain hidden, possibly a gift of money from a dubious source, or a bribe or some other kind of payment for an illicit act, possibly with sexual connections. When there is a question concerning human relationships, Peorth indicates one based only on sexual attraction between the partners, which is liable to be shorter-lived than one based on other areas of compatibility. More generally, this rune refers to sexual compatibility and sexual secrets kept between partners. Esoterically, the rune can indicate initiation, or hidden, inner, inexplicable experiences: paranormal events, or mediumistic contact with the otherworld, either through conscious effort or by "chance." The outcome of these experiences will be to the querent's benefit, and personal growth will be the result.

With the Peorth card inverted, events are not likely to happen the way the querent would like them to. Hopes will not be fulfilled. The querent may expect unpleasant surprises and non-beneficial secrets coming to light. One may discover that they are suffering from an illness, perhaps not curable by orthodox medicine. Spiritually, caution is indicated with the inverted Peorth card, for there is the possibility that any of the querent's disciplines involving altered states of consciousness may get out of control. More generally, this reading warns against potentially disastrous outcomes from experimenting with that which is not quite controlled or understood. An inverted Peorth rune indicates that the querent may be susceptible to dependency on alcohol or drugs. Taking chances in any field is unwise now: it is likely to lead to disaster.

The querent is warned against any involvement in untried or uncertain schemes, specifically gambling, speculating, or lending money—it is very likely that any investment will be lost completely.

Peorth inverted also reveals bad things that others have perpetrated covertly against the querent, perhaps leading to break-ups of friendships or one's marriage. This reading denotes bad publicity, perhaps in the form of "skeletons in the closet"—such as an unpleasant hidden past being discovered by colleagues or the press.

EIWAZ

Old German: Algiz, Elhaz; Gothic, Algs;
Anglo-Saxon: Eolh, Eolhx; Old Norse: Ihwar, Man.

The fifteenth rune is named Eiwaz (Elhaz or Eolh). The card depicts a tree with upraised arms, guarding the landscape against hidden forces that manifest in the shape of threatening Yarthkins (malevolent earth spirits and rock-demons, also known as trolls). Their ugly grimaces can be perceived in the rocks to the right of the tree. To the left of the tree, protected from the demonic forces by the power of Eiwaz, is an altar-like rock. Behind the tree and over the altar-rock shines an unearthly amber-colored light, the amber stone that corresponds to the rune. In front of the Eiwaz tree floats a bubble, signifying the connecting or merging of different states, the unifying "third possibility" between polarities.

The Old German and Anglo-Saxon versions of this rune signify the elk. Its spiky, defensive form represents the power of resistance inherent in the mighty antlers of the elk, and the protective "warding off" sign of the splayed hand. Its Gothic interpretation is thought to refer to a swan, another fiercely defensive creature. Eiwaz is one of the most benevolent runes; its name is derived from the Old German word *algiz*, which means "protection." Protection, then, is the prime significance of this rune. More specifically, Eiwaz represents the defensive power of the elk, the power of resistance symbolized by its mighty antlers. It is the rune sacred to the defender-god Heimdall, the guardian of the rainbow bridge Bifröst, the link between earth and sky, the human and the heavenly. Heimdall, in his guise as Rig, was the legendary organizer of the three ranks of ancient society. He is the guardian of the stronghold of the gods, and the old Gothic word *alhs,* meaning "sanctuary," is related to the meaning of this rune. In northern Europe, the yew tree, with which this rune is connected, is a marker of sacred places, especially churches which stand on the sites of former heathen places of power. The form of the rune is that of a person standing in the position of prayer and exultation; and in the later Scandinavian rune-rows, it is called Man. Constructionally, the later Man rune is related to the rune of the same name in the Elder Futhark by contraction into the form of the earlier Eiwaz.

Eiwaz represents the striving of human consciousness ever upward toward enlightenment, or from the material level toward the spiritual. Symbolically, this is the solar power imminent between the antlers of the elk, the sunwheel, or the third eye of enlightened consciousness. Such enlightenment is a link between the earthly and the divine. In the sacred traditions of many cultures, this link is personified as the Divine Twins, one earthly and one heavenly, sometimes also depicted as male and female. The earth-heaven link is present in the Greco-Roman tradition as the great god Pan and his Celtic counterpart Cernunnos, the horned god, guardian of all wild animals. In the mysteries of the Celtic druids, this rune is the sacred sigil composed of three lines, called the *Awen*. It is the most sacred sign of druidism, representing the spark of genius descending from the sun, symbol of the Allfather or godhead. It is the light of inspiration, representing the triadic or threefold nature of all things. Its symbolic color is gold, and its precious stone is amber, the "Stone of Victory," used in former times for magical protection. As the medieval Gaelic ballad, *Seurlus an Dobhair* ("The King of Bergen's Son") tells us: "...On the maiden's fingers, there was found the gold, fashioned like gameboard squares, and there were nine sets of the stones of victory on each side of her ring...." These nine amber stones were there to invoke the protective power implicit in Eiwaz, "by the power of three times three."

With Eiwaz, this inspiration operates in a protective way. It is a rune of awareness. If there is any danger, this rune indicates that the querent will intuitively know of it and be able to avert disaster. It signifies the quality of rising above adversity, much as a tree rises above the rocks among which it has take root. The Anglo-Saxon version of this rune has the meaning of the elk-sedge (elongated sedge), a hardy and resistant plant which grows in the wetlands of East Anglia in eastern England. The Old English Rune Poem describes it thus: "Elk-sedge grows mainly in fenlan, flourishing in the water, grimly wounds, burning with the blood of anyone who tries to grip it." Eiwaz promises a ready protection and even a counter-offensive against those powers and influences with which we find ourselves in conflict.

The element associated with Eiwaz is air. As a defensive rune, Eiwaz is ruled by Heimdall, the watcher-god. In the tarot, Eiwaz is associated with trump XV, The Devil. The Haindl Tarot, also by Hermann Haindl, does not offer the dualistic personified view of the principle of evil, but instead portrays the eternal strength and power of nature. This principle is also recognized in R. J. Stewart's Merlin Tarot, where his equivalent trump is called The Guardian, and is represented by the antler-wearing figure of the Lord of the Forest, personified as Herne the Hunter or Cernunnos, the God of the Witches. Eiwaz is the rune of the first spring festival of Imbolc or Brigantia (February 1). The traditional sigil of this festival, used on farmers' calendars, is derived from the rune. The rune rules the half-month from January 28 until February 12.

In a runic reading, the upright form of Eiwaz is a most optimistic, powerful, and benevolent sign. It signifies protection, a successful defense of the querent's will against negative influences. It is the rune of warding off all harm, the power of the elk and of amber, signifying the cure and healing of illness. Eiwaz specifies the resolution of any problems in question in a manner favorable to the querent. One will be reconciled with one's opponents without losing to them. When the question concerns a relationship, Eiwaz denotes concord and stability within an existing partnership, and, where there are problems at present, reconciliation. A new relationship with a good-natured person may also be indicated.

Inverted, the rune warns of a lack of protection and vulnerability to attack from every quarter. The querent may want something to which he or she is not entitled. Deception is likely, with the querent as the victim. In this, there may be elements of willingness to be deceived. This inverted card also indicates the possibility of the querent becoming a victim of the nefarious activities of others, perhaps even being made a scapegoat for something he or she has not done. Inverted, Eiwaz has strong elements of sacrifice, downfall, even death; though this, like the Death card of the tarot, may be interpreted as radical change.

Inverted, Eiwaz takes on the same external form as Yr. However, in this card version of the runes, the inverted Eiwaz is definitely not the same as the upright Yr. In the Scandinavian rune-row, the inverted version of this rune (which is called MannaR, written with a final capital "R") is a magical rune which signifies the final letter "R" or "Z" on Norse words like UngandiR (meaning "unaffected by magical attack"). In the Northern Tradition, the Eiwaz rune has also been used to denote a person's dates of birth and death. The upright form of Eiwaz signifies a birthdate, while its inversion is said to represent the date of someone's demise. The symbol of nuclear disarmament, which appears to be an inverted Eiwaz ("the death rune"), was in fact designed by an English advertising agency in the 1950s. It was derived from the military semaphore letters "N" and "D", for Nuclear Disarmament. According to rune-mistress Freya Aswynn, the upright form of this rune denotes the male, and the inverted denotes the female, so the polarity of the rune is dual.

SIG

Old German, Sowulo; Gothic, Saúil; Anglo-Saxon, Sigel; Old Norse, Sól.

The sixteenth rune of the Elder Futhark, the last stave of the ætt of Hagal, is Sig. In all versions, the names mean "sun." Hermann Haindl's card painting depicts Sig as the devastatingly powerful flash of lightning energy that links the two polar opposites of Earth and sky. This spectacular electrical discharge unifies momentarily the female energy of Mother Earth and the male solar power. The rune Sig primarily reflects the principle of polarity. In a rune reading, it signifies triumphant success. When its shape symbolism is examined, it appears as the flash of lightning. As the irresistible power of lightning, Sig is linked conceptually with Dorn, for lightning can sweep away everything literally in a flash. This dangerous aspect of Sig has been used deliberately as a means of gaining power and domination over others. But, as with everything else in the universe, misuse of a magic sigil brings its own retribution and the inevitable restoration of balance by bringing destruction upon those who misused it.

Traditionally, this rune symbolizes the stupendous power of the sun and the vital qualities of daylight. In the earliest religions, the sun was worshipped—rightly—as the source of life itself. Sunwheels appear on the earliest Alpine and Scandinavian rock-carvings; later, solar deities such as Amun-Re, Ormazd, Helios, Apollo, Ogmios, Helith, Balder, Quetzalcoatl, Kukulkán, and Ameratasu were numbered among the chief deities of various civilizations. The sun is the source of most of the energy reaching the earth, and, ultimately, it is the source of most of the energy in fossil fuels. Without the sun's power, there would be no life on earth at all, and certainly no conscious civilization that could recognize and celebrate the fact.

The Old English Rune Poem describes the quality of Sig as: "To seafarers, when they sail across the fishes' bath, the Sun always means hope, until the horse of the sea brings them to their haven." Here, the poem describes both the sun itself and the clear attainment of goals that the rune signifies. Symbolically, this rune is the magical will acting beneficially throughout the world, sustaining life. This positive attainment can be manifested on either the physical level or on the divine. Sig signifies that irresistible, ultimately solar power, which can vanquish all opposition—the undefeated sun—the Sol Invictus celebrated at the Roman midwinter festival of the same name, the northern Yuletide.

In the battle between light and darkness, light will always be victorious. The Northern Tradition tells of two aspects of the sun, described as the goddesses Sól and Sunna: "Among men, she is called Sól; and among the Gods, Sunna," states The Elder Edda. According to Edred Thorsson, Sól is the name of the phenomenon, while Sunna signifies the spiritual power of solar energy. Sunna, manifested in Sig, is that selfless spiritual quality which counters the forces of death and disintegration. Sól is the goddess who rides in the chariot of the sun, while Sunna drives it. Here is a link between the runes Sig and Rit, where Sig is the ruling spiritual power in control, and Rit is the act of control under the spiritual force.

Secondary meanings of both of these runes are different aspects of the sunwheel, the Hvel or Hweol. This is the sunwheel, the cyclic wheel of time, wheel of fortune, etc., that links to the subtle wheels within the body, the chakras of Hindu tradition which are intimately linked with the individual's self-development. The solar wheel also has another meaning: that of the sun wagon. Again, the early Bronze Age sun wagon from Trundholm in Zealand, Denmark, links the sun with the horse. It seems that in early runic tradition, the sun and the horse had a close esoteric connection, giving a link between the runes Sig and Ehwaz, guidance, and maintaining a course. Symbolically, the guidance across the sea that the sun affords seafarers, according to the Old English Rune Poem, is the light of experience and the inner light of wisdom that can guide us in life.

Sig's gender is male; its primary element is air, but it is also linked to fire and water. In the Northern Tradition, it is ruled over by the summer sun god Balder as well as the solar goddesses Sól and Sunna. In ancient Holland, the goddess Barbet was the solar deity. In later times, she was worshipped as Saint Barbara, who had assimilated her attributes. But in most cultures, the main attribute of the sun is in the male gender, as opposed to the female nature of earth. Here, the Sig rune is the herald of triumphant ascendancy of light over darkness, using the power of the sun for guidance and healing.

Sig is the seventh non-invertible rune. But it can be "handed." In other words, there can be a mirror image. Freya Aswynn believes that the common form is left-handed, so its mirror image is the right-handed form. This makes the common form male and the mirror-image form female. They can be seen as extrovert and introvert forms of the rune. The male or left-handed rune sends power out-wards, while conversely, the opposite form draws it in.

Commonly, however, only one form of the rune is used: that which is depicted on the card. In a runecast, Sig promises unexpected success in a venture, often accompanied by a sudden and spectacular failure of all opposition. Because it signifies self-direction along the path of one's true will, Sig indicates that the querent will enjoy almost limitless energy, a powerful life force channeled toward the achievement of one's objectives. In a venture, there will be a fortunate successful outcome. As it refers to the life force, Sig points toward radiant good health and strength. Generally, Sig denotes that matters in question are running well and are "on course." The querent should continue to proceed in an unchanged manner with regard to matters in question. But if Sig falls in combination with unfortunate, delay-indicating runes, such as reversed Dorn, Hagal, Not, Is, etc., Sig indicates that the subject is likely to worry about problems and thus delay any action that might be necessary to deal with them.

An inverted Sig rune card does not indicate bad luck or other setbacks, but it is less beneficial than the upright card. It can indicate that the querent is an obsessive worker, a person who does not know how to relax. Emotional problems could come as a result of this sort of energy flow, perhaps the break-up of relationships, or long-term health problems. In matters of health, reversed Sig indicates that the querent is liable to overdo, leading to burn-out. Overall, whatever the reading, Sig will indicate the most positive actions possible under the circumstances.

TYR

Old German, Teiwaz; Gothic, Teiws; Anglo-Saxon, Tir; Norse, Tyr.

The spear or arrow-shaped Tyr is the seventeenth rune. Hermann Haindl's rune card depicts a scene in a forest at night. The setting is a high point in the landscape, a small clearing with rocks, deep within the forest. A guiding star can be seen shining through the trees, and on one of the boulders at the foot of the Tyr-tree itself is engraved a large, tight spiral. It is an ideal location for Otiseta, the Northern Tradition spiritual exercise of "sitting out," the European equivalent of Eastern meditations and the Native American vision quest. Only the lower part of the tree is visible, but the unseen upper part could well reach to the stars. Spiritually, an upward motion from the heavens above the tree is suggested.

This is the first rune of the third ætt, called the ætt of Tyr. The literal meaning of the rune in all versions is that of the god Tyr himself. The rune's shape expresses the conscious targeting of positive forces for the greatest effect. It can be seen both as a symbol of physical conflict, and as the vault of the heavens arching over the cosmic axis, the covering branches of the tree protecting the world beneath it. The rune is named after the god Tyr, whose name means, basically, "universal father," or "god." Hence, it signifies eternal stability. When Odin is seen as an aspect of the All-Father, several of his by-names end in Tyr: Hangatyr ("The Hanged God"); Veratyr ("God of Men"). The name "Tyr" comes from the ancient Indo-European set of cognate words for "god." They are related to the Sanskrit word *dayus*, which has the meaning of "a god or divine spirit." From this comes the name of the Greek chief god Zeus, the Roman Dis-Pater (Jupiter), and the Latin word for God, *Deus*. The ancient Indo-European sky god, worshipped in archaic times in Europe, is believed to have borne a name something like *deivos*, which later developed into Teiwaz, Tîw, or Ziu, and then, in the Norse countries, into Tyr. To the Celts, he was Teutates, assimilated with Mars by the Roman conquerors of Gaul and Britain. The Christian religion, in overthrowing the worship of this aspect of the Allfather, transferred the name "Teiwaz" to its anti-god, the Devil.

As a deity and as a rune, however, Tyr is the principle of right order in the cosmos. As the rune of the divine ruler, Tyr signifies positive regulation, stability, protection, and success. But in Tyr, success is accompanied by loss, for there can be no success without personal sacrifice. The northern divinity Tyr is sometimes equated with the Roman god Mars. In English, the day-name Tuesday recalls the Anglo-Saxon version of the god's name, Tiw. This god was the patronal deity of the Swabians, and Augsburg once known as Ziusburg, their capital. Tübingen, too, is a city dedicated to Tyr. In England, where he was one of the major divinities worshipped by Anglo-Saxon pagans, his sacred animal was the red horse, carved into a hillside at Tysoe in Warwickshire. This rune can be considered especially powerful at those places.

As a rune, Tyr has great power. It symbolizes one aspect of the cosmic axis, the sacred world pillar Irminsul, with the vault of the heavens above it. Irming or Ermin is a by-name of Tyr. It is also significant in its aspect as the tree of measure (or justice), the gallows. In former times, the major place of execution of outlaws and highwaymen in England was at a crossroads sacred to Tyr, just outside the City of London. It was the triangular gallows known as the "triple tree" at Tyburn, which means literally "the burn or brook of the god Tyr." The site is now named after the triumphal Marble Arch, a major traffic intersection. As a link between the worlds, Tyr as the cosmic axis maintains order, as the gallows was thought to do in former times. Thus, the rune Tyr can be said to correspond with The Hanged Man of the tarot (trump XII).

Tyr is a rune allied to the male polarity, which is ruled by the element air. Tyr is the most courageous and victorious aspect of the gods; he surpasses others and does not waver. In ancient northern Europe, Tyr was the name given to a star. Although it is not certain, it is probable that Tyr was the pole star, the marker of the top of the cosmic axis, the star which does not appear to move when all others do. The Old English Rune Poem accounts for it thus: "Tir is a special mark, it keeps faith with noblemen, it is always on course through the darkness of night. It never turns aside." Here, Tyr represents an unfailingly true guiding star, which can be nothing other than the pole star, known today by its astronomical name of Polaris, or its traditional appellation of "The Nail." Perhaps the poem also refers to the compass needle, the magnetized iron that is always on course, pointing the way. Iron is the metal ruled by Tyr and his equivalent, the Roman god Mars. Both are gods of combat and glory.

Strength, constancy, and steadfast reliability are perhaps the rune's most important attributes. The form of the rune Tyr is related directly to the astrological sigil for the planet Mars. In this form, it signifies the competitive, combative spirit and the active, masculine principle. Tyr is a rune of protection, which was used by the warriors of former times to assist them in battle by magically preventing death or serious wounds. Correspondingly, its sacred herbs are those of battlefield wortcunning (herb lore): sage, that of the purifying incense, producer of an antiseptic salve; and the poisonous herb aconite, Tyr's Helm. In former times, the juice of this latter herb, a potent nerve poison, was used on arrows. But, in the hands of an expert herbalist, the products of Tyr's Helm can also be used to alleviate pain, and was used to treat wounded warriors. This herbal paradox is also associated with the rune Peorth.

The major divinatory meaning of this rune, that there can be no success without some form of loss, can be understood with reference to the legend of the Fenris-Wolf. This supernatural wolf, offspring of the trickster-god Loki, was brought to Asgard, the abode of the Norse gods and goddesses, as a pup. But even then, it was so fearsome that only Tyr had the courage to approach it closely enough to feed it. But soon the wolf grew so large that it began to threaten the cosmic order. So the gods decided to bind the wolf and cast it into the underworld. They tried to fool the wolf by pretending that the binding was a game to test its strength. But the wolf was aware of what was happening, and was aware, too, that no ordinary bonds could tie him. In the first two attempts, the bonds were so weak that the mighty wolf was able to break them easily. Then the gods ordered a third, magical bond called Gleipnir, which was fashioned for them by the Dark Elves from six magically paradoxical or difficult-to-obtain things: the noise a cat makes when it moves; the beard of a woman; the roots of a mountain; the sinews of a bear; the breath of a fish; and the spittle of a bird. Armed with Gleipnir, the gods took the wolf to an island called Lyngvi to test him. On its third binding, Tyr assured the wolf that it would be released after the test. But the wolf, fearing trickery, demanded that one of the gods should put his right hand in his mouth as a sign of good faith, that, should the fetter prove unbreakable, then they would remove it from the wolf. Only Tyr was brave enough to put his hand between the wolf's jaws. The wolf was bound, and when it was clear that the Æsir would not free the wolf, Fenris bit off Tyr's right hand at the wrist, a place that became known in the Northern Tradition as the "wolf-joint." By sacrificing his hand,

Tyr saved the gods from destruction by the otherwise invincible supernatural wolf.

The rune Tyr thus symbolizes the valor and bravery required to be a spiritual warrior, the necessary willingness to sacrifice one's most treasured possessions in order to restore balance. Tyr is the rune of the will, of single-minded motivation, the devoted support of a cause. It is the power to continue in the face of difficulties. But in Tyr the will must be motivated by fairness and not by personal greed, with the recognition that one must take full responsibility for one's own actions. This recognition is one of spiritual enlightenment, which is trusting in the benevolence of the right orderliness of the universe. As the old god Tîwaz, this was the essence of the Sky Father who mated with the Earth Mother to bring fertility to the world. Appropriately, the next rune, Bar, is the rune of the Earth Mother, patroness of mothers and their children. In relation to appropriate questions, the rune Tyr indicates physical attraction, successful sexual relationships, and emotional happiness.

In magic and divination, Tyr is a rune which controls positive regulation. This often shows itself as that self-sacrifice which is required for one to rule justly. In the upright divinatory position, Tyr indicates success, but that it will involve self-sacrifice. The rune can indicate success in competition in all places where contests for position take place: work interviews, sporting contests, examinations, or competitive bids for business contracts. Tyr is lord of judgment, the ruler of legal proceedings, tests, and competition in business transactions or personal relationships. When favorably positioned, it signifies an increase in personal power. The rune may indicate legal proceedings, either initiated by the querent (if upright) or by others (inverted), but the outcome will only be favorable if the querent has right on his or her side. Miscarriages of justice will not occur with Tyr, even if they are favorable to the querent. Tyr is the rune of the god of justice, which must also apply to the judge as well as the judged. But whatever the outcome, Tyr tells us that it must be borne with courage and fortitude.

Tyr is an invertible rune, whose inversion indicates the absence of or negation of the positive qualities of Tyr. When reversed in a reading, Tyr warns that the querent is liable to give up in the face of difficulties. This is the result of blockages to the natural flow of events, which must be dealt with if progress is to be made. A blockage may be manifested in frustrated love, marital difficulties, emotional problems, and/or legal troubles. Tyr can also denote impatience in the querent. But this rune instructs us not to give up the quest: all things will work out in the end according to cosmic law, for Tyr signifies those qualities necessary for the spiritual warrior.

Generally, the inverted rune can be interpreted as the waning of one's power, perhaps manifested as a loss of former enthusiasm or drive. Sexually, this can appear as lack of fidelity, frustrated love, marital unhappiness, flagging sexual powers, or general sexual and emotional problems. Traditionally, the inverted Tyr rune has been associated with death in battle; but in spiritual terms, it may indicate the death of a worldly life, and a rebirth on the spiritual level. On every level, Tyr is the aim of the quest: spiritual enlightenment.

BAR

Old German, Berkana; Gothic, Baírkan;
Anglo-Saxon, Beorc; Old Norse, Bairkan.

The mysterious eighteenth rune is Bar. The rune card depicts the Great Goddess, Mother Earth, as the body of a woman lying on the ground. Above her, in the sky, is the constellation of the virgin, and the moon, which in Native American cultures represents the grandmother principle. To the right, the side of the conscious mind, is the white-barked trunk and branches of the sacred birch tree. Here, Bar signifies the mother who gives all to us. Her great mystery is that simultaneously she gives birth to life and death.

Traditionally, this rune represents the birch tree, but it is better known as the rune of the Great Mother Goddess. The Old German and Old Norse forms are versions of the name of the Birch Goddess, while the Gothic form means "a twig of the birch tree." Its Anglo-Saxon form also refers to the birch tree. The birch is symbolic of purity and purification, but Bar· is also the rune of mystery, the mystery being that of birth, life, and death—generation and regeneration. As the birch, the first tree which grew on the barren land after the retreat of the ice cap at the end of the last Ice Age, this rune is symbolic of rebirth. The Old English Rune Poem states: "The Birch bears no fruit, yet it shoots without seeding, has shining branches high in its ornamented helmet, laden with leaves, touching the sky."

In its shape, the fecund, feminine, rune Bar echoes the breasts of the Earth Mother Goddess, Berchta (Bertha, who is also celebrated with slightly variant attributes by the names of Nerthus, Erda, Frigg, Holda, Frau Gode, The White Lady, and Ostara). Of course, the element ascribed to Bar is earth. Bar is the rune ruling women's menstrual periods, pregnancy, and birth, but also governs the relationship between parents and children. An important attribute of Berchta is that she gives shelter to and protects abandoned children. In legend, Berchta watches over agriculture and horticulture, caring for the plants. Each of her entourage of children carries a little jar of water for the plants. In her hollow, twin-peaked holy mountain, she nurtures the unmanifested souls who are to be brought into the world as new children. Her apparition is considered to herald great prosperity for the beholder.

In the tradition of the Celtic Oghams, Bar as the birch tree is the first character of the "tree alphabet," Beth. The tree of the White Goddess and the sun god Belenos marks the springtime rebirth of the sun's vigor. Although it is classified as a "kiln" or "peasant" tree, and not considered a "noble" tree, the birch is nevertheless the prime tree of the Celts. It is the tree of rebirth, with twigs used as a charm for fruitfulness among animals and humans. An early custom was to bury the dead wearing a hat made of birch bark. Similarly, in the traditional English ballad, *The Wife of Usher's Well,* her three slain sons, returning as ghosts, wear birch hats: "The carlin wife's three sons came home, and their hats were of the bird…" The birch is the tree of purification, used to expel all bad thoughts and influences, to herald a new beginning.

In many places, the trunk of the birch forms the maypole. The twigs of the birch are used to make the brush of the Wiccan besom; according to tradition, sweeping the ground around the house with the birch twigs of the besom forms a psychic barrier against all evil.

In one of its Norse versions, Bjorg, this rune signifies the sacred snow-covered twin hills which exist as holy mountains of the goddess all over Europe and in other continents. This is also symbolized by the highest point of the rainbow, Heimdall's palace, Himinbjorg. Between these twin peaks, the sun rises or sets at certain significant times of the year. The crystal or glass mountain of Celtic tradition is a version of this—Caer Sidhe, the Fairy Mountain. Ancient sacred places of the goddess, such as Newgrange in Ireland, were covered once in white quartz crystals, becoming the White Hills of legend. The holy mountain of the goddess Holda, Venusberg, is another version. In her aspect as Holda, the goddess also guards the holy well called Quickborn, from which flow the waters of birth and rejuvenation.

As Bar, the rune is related to the Northern Tradition martial arts cult of the bear, whose tutelary goddess, another aspect of the Great Mother Goddess, was known to the Celts as Artio. One of her major shrines was near the Swiss city of Bern, whose foundation came as the result of a vision of the bear goddess in her animal form. The city's coat of arms still carries the brown bear of the goddess. The devotees of the bear cult were the much-feared Berserkers.

Finally, Bar can also be seen as the bier upon which the dead were carried to their funerals, paralleling the solar barque of ancient Egyptian tradition. Adherents to that religion saw death not as the end of life, but the beginning of a new one in the Otherworld. Bar is the name of the soul-bird in the ancient Egyptian culture. In classical European tradition, this function is assumed by Charon, the ferryman who transports souls from one world to the other. In the Northern Tradition, this is ascribed to the goddess Mordgud.

Bar, as the eighteenth rune, has a number double that of the sacred nine of Hagal. In Northern Tradition numerology, the number eighteen indicates new beginnings on a higher level. This is one of the Northern Tradition numbers of completion, signifying that point where the underlying principles have come into being and are fully established. New forms can then come to fruition within the framework already set up. In the annual runic time cycle, Bar rules the half-month from March 14 until March 30, which includes the day of the Vernal Equinox. Magically, then, this rune lies liturgically in the east, the point at which many circle ceremonies commence.

In divination, Bar is a rune of physical beginnings. Bar is the Biarg-rune, a rune of fecundity. It signifies a birth, whether the physical birth of a baby, or the conceptual birth of an idea, or the physical inception of a business project. It indicates that any ideas which the subject may have been considering should be put into action without delay. In a runecast, Bar signifies a time of new growth, encouraging the inquirer to expand or expedite any project in question. Bar indicates that such a project will have a good result, even though, like a newborn baby, it may need some nurturing before coming to maturity. More generally, new beginnings of all kinds are indicated. This can mean the formation of new relationships, an engagement, or marriage. It can point toward a matter concerning the querent's mother. Because Bar signifies the caring, maternal influence, if the subject is expecting a child, it is a fortunate omen when this rune occurs in the upright position. In general, Bar is a good rune for anything to do with nurturing and growth.

When the card is reversed, Bar indicates cessation of growth. It should be taken as a warning of impending problems—but these problems are avoidable. Bar tells of the present genesis of problems which can be prevented or mitigated if dealt with swiftly. In a relationship, this inverted rune signifies stagnation, perhaps ending in separation or divorce if nothing is done about it. It can also presage disharmony within the family. In business, it denotes failure, especially of new businesses. When connected with pregnancy, Bar reversed warns of the possibility of miscarriage or stillbirth, if preventative steps are not taken. Wherever bad outcomes are indicated, they are warnings to be heeded, but not as the result of unavoidable processes. An inverted Bar card urges the inquirer to be prepared for avertable problems and to seek some practical means of evading them.

ehwaz

Old German, Ehwaz; Gothic, Egeis; Anglo-Saxon, Eh; Old Norse, Ior.

The nineteenth rune, with the literal meaning of "a horse," is Ehwaz. This rune card shows one beech tree and one oak tree standing side by side. They are connected by a branch that, like an arm, seeks to touch the other. Oaks are water-seeking trees, while beeches are not. Although the two are discordant trees, through the agency of the third, forked tree, they become united harmoniously. It is as though by lifting both of its "arms," this third tree has united the two apparent opposites. Seemingly incorporeal horses and other animals arise from the background and from within the trees themselves. These remind us of the friendship between humans and animals, and, more specifically, of Sleipnir, the supernatural horse of Odin. The eyes in the trees look at us especially strongly, appealing to us to protect and strengthen our friendship or partnership with the trees and the animals of this planet: we are truly one with them. As the Native American holy man Chief Seattle wisely said in the last century, "What you do to animals and trees, you do to yourselves."

All of the traditional meanings of this rune name refer to the horse. The alternative Old German version of the rune's name Ehwaz means "the two horses," while the Gothic form means "stallion." The Anglo-Saxon variant has the meaning of "a war horse." The Old English Rune Poem gives the reading for this rune as: "The horse is the joy of one's equals, stepping out with pride. When it is talked about all around by wealthy riders, and to the restless, it is always a comfort." The horse is numbered among the most sacred animals of the Elder Faith of Northern Europe. It is associated with sky gods and goddesses, symbolically pulling the wagons of the sun and moon. There are ancient representations of this, such as the famous sun wagon from Trundholm, Zealand, Denmark. Here, the horse signifies the cosmic order in the shape of the course of the sun and moon in the heavens. In Norse cosmology, the wain of the goddess Sól was pulled by two horses, Aarvakr, "Early-Waker," and Alsvin, "Rapid-Goer." These horses are recalled by traditional double horse and horse-head carvings, sometimes accompanied by a sun wheel, on house gables in Germany and Scandinavia. The lunar steed was called Alsvider, "Il-Swift," while the black horse which drew the dark car of Nott, goddess of night, was pulled by Hrimfaxi, "Frist-Mane," from whose mane dew and frost dropped upon the earth by night. The chariot of Dag, the god of day, by contrast, was drawn by the white horse, Skinfaxi, "Shining-Mane."

Ehwaz also refers to Sleipnir, the eight-legged steed of Odin, a personification in animal form of the shaman's means of travel to other worlds. In certain parts of southern England, especially Kent, there is a tradition that involves groups of men processing through villages at Midwinter carrying a wooden horse's head known as the "Hoodening Horse." *Hoodening* is a word cognate with *Woden,* the Saxon name for Odin, and so the horse represents Sleipnir. In Wales, a horse's skull known as Mari Lwyd is dressed up and carried about by a man enveloped in a cloak. The horse's jaws are snapped as he dances about, visiting the houses of the village, demanding food and drink. These practices at midwinter are reminders that the horse and the sun are intimately linked in European folk tradition. The white horse was the standard of the Saxons, and in Kent, the white horse is still the totemic animal. This White Horse of Kent is depicted traditionally with men attempting to catch and bind him with ropes, but he breaks free and is called Invictus, the Undefeated. This was also one of the traditional titles of the sun—Sol Invictus, the old Roman name for the Yuletide festivities of midwinter. Symbolic white horses are still to be seen carved on hillsides in southern England.

In former times, the skull of the horse was a magical object, being used both as a means of cursing enemies and as a protector of buildings against all kinds of harm. When used to curse, a horse's skull was set on a pole known as a Niodstong. Mal-runes and Swart-runes were carved on the post, and it was set at a place of power facing the enemy's house. Its function was to disturb the Landvættir, or earth spirits, where the enemy lived, creating such psychic turmoil that the enemy would be forced to leave. Traditional Russian magic teaches that a special ambrosia issues from the horse's head, which enables its possessor to do exceptional deeds. When used as a magical protection, a horse's skull was buried in the foundations of a building. This practice was widespread formerly in Germany, Holland, and England. The known last example of this practice in England took place in 1895 at Black Horse Drove near Cambridge. There, the builders poured a libation of ale over the skull, laid as a foundation for a Methodist Chapel.

Like the next rune, Man, Ehwaz is one of combination. It is associated with the bond between the horse and its rider, or horses harnessed to a wagon, and, more tenuously, between human twins, brotherhood and sisterhood. The rune's written form is a bind-rune of two mirror-image Lagu runes, inferring the union of the flow of the conscious and unconscious, and of the male and female principles. Ehwaz symbolizes the qualities of absolute trust and loyalty necessary in those who undertake a sacred journey. This applies equally to following a spiritual path, or, more literally, to a physical expedition in a pilgrimage or seer's journey. Ehwaz assists one in keeping control of the emotions, which is a necessary skill for those who would undertake the way of spiritual or magical attainment. On a more general level, Ehwaz represents that motion necessary to undertake any task. It is the task of life which our Wyrd has brought us, and which must be tackled with fortitude. Ehwaz is ruled by the goddess Freyja, and the gods Frey and Odin. The element of earth is connected with Ehwaz, which has both polarities, feminine and masculine.

Ehwaz is an invertible rune, and so there can be an upright and a reversed meaning. Upright, Ehwaz refers to the physical, legal, spiritual, and magical links between people. As a rune connected with sexuality, Ehwaz can refer to a mutually enriching and long-lasting sexual relationship. In appropriate circumstances, it can indicate the likelihood of marriage. Ehwaz indicates a journey, especially by land, or a change involving travel, such as moving house. When the question is spiritual, Ehwaz symbolizes the beginning of a psychic journey; or more prosaically, an alteration in lifestyle. Ehwaz points out that, to achieve one's objectives, one must enter an undertaking which will involve coming together with a reliable partner for a fruitful partnership. As with any joint venture, this will involve adjustments, give-and-take, but the querent will be capable of taking control of the situation and handling it to everyone's advantage.

Reversed, Ehwaz expresses some negative elements, but not a complete reversal of its upright meaning. It can refer to the loosening or breaking of bonds between individuals, distancing in both the figurative and physical senses. The Ehwaz rune inverted signifies restlessness or failed journeys. This can refer to attempts to move house which are thwarted at the last moment through deceit or trickery. More generally, Ehwaz designates the likelihood of sudden and unexpected change, its outcome depending on accompanying runes in the runecast. It refers to the possibility of broken relationships, the discovery of false friends. Generally, inverted, this rune warns the querent that, so far as may be possible, things should not be changed at present. But where relationships end or falsehood is exposed, the lessons learned by the querent can be turned to future advantage.

ᛗᚨᚾ

Old German, Mannaz; Gothic, Manna; Anglo-Saxon, Man; Old Norse, Madhr.

The twentieth rune is Man, or Mannaz. Hermann Haindl's rune card depicts the Man rune as a grouping of two trees: one red and one blue. This symbolizes the polar nature of humanity in both genders and within each individual. The two trees are forked, crossing their arm-branches, making the form of the "present rune," Gebo. Individually, each tree takes the form of a Kan rune. Therefore, in its written form, the rune Man can be seen as a bind-rune composed of two Kan runes. These are mirror images of one another, signifying the integration of the intuitive wisdom of the right side with the conscious wisdom of the left. Here, the card shows that Man can also be interpreted as a different bind-rune. It is composed of two Lagu runes, linking the ingoing with the outgoing, and the unconscious flow of things with its conscious aspects. Spiritually, this double bind-rune signifies the human being in his and her landscape, humankind in balance with our environment. Behind and above the trees, the skies open solemnly. Above, some clouds are illuminated by the light of a reddish sun. Below, the depths are lit by a yellow light, giving a presentiment of a wide landscape. At the left is the foxglove plant, which produces digitalin, a substance which can be poisonous, but when used in correct dosages may be used as an important heart medication. If we use nature's products appropriately and with reverence, then we may bring happiness to humanity.

In all versions, this rune denotes the basic reality of being human which is present in all of us, whether male or female. It is the shared experience of every person's human condition that affirms our common humanity. The Old English Rune Poem reminds us that, "A man in happiness is dear to his kindred, yet each must depart from one another, because the gods will commit their flesh to the ground." This rune affirms the common solidarity of all human beings, whatever their age, gender, race, nationality, or religion. The Man rune, like the human species, has both gender polarities. The secondary influences upon the rune are from Odin and his consort, Frigg.

Man is primarily a Hug rune, a rune of the mind which controls mental ability and verbal communication. In this aspect, the Man rune is related to things concerning the mind, such as discussions, debates, arguments, legal disputes, academic examinations, in general, stating one's case, when it serves as a Mal-rune. As a rune of linking, it governs intellectual compatibility and enhances mutual understanding. In its written form, the rune Man represents the archetypal human being, Man the Microcosm, as the reflection of all things natural. Our conscious position in nature is a special one, and all of us as humans have the same responsibility to the earth on which we walk, the mother of us all. The divine attribute of the Man rune, as with Hagal, is the god Heimdall. Heimdall, according to legend, under his by-name of Rig, was the progenitor of the traditional classes of ancient European society. Here, Man is symbolically the embodiment of the social order, without which our full potential as human beings is unattainable. The geometry of the rune is of two Wunjo runes conjoined, representing the joy of male and female together, and the true human potential of the linking of the conscious and sub-conscious. In the best human relationships, we are in a win-win situation, where both parties gain and none loses.

As an upright rune card in a divination, Man signifies win-win situations: a good life in harmony with one's surroundings. The nature of the Man rune as a bind-rune of Kan and its mirror-image indicates a proper, balanced frame of mind in which the conscious and the unconscious are in an appropriate relationship with one another. The power of integrated thought and intuition are denoted, bringing the ability to make a good judgment of the situation in ques-tion. Inverted, the Man rune indicates solitary actions. The querent may feel cut off from other people, and may even have the tendency to cut themselves off deliberately, refusing the advice or assistance of others. Thus, inverted Man denotes that there will be no outside help in dealing with the matter in question. In addition, the inquirer's intuition and conscious thought are out of harmony with one another, leading to confusion and ineffectiveness. Obstruction of one's plans is indicated. This is likely to be the result of officialdom, bureaucracy, or individual enemies. Subversion of one's activities by others should be expected. But as Man reversed signifies that one's selfishness rules one's actions, negative attitudes may lead to refusal of help from the one source which could prevent disaster. However, this selfishness is likely to be so badly directed that it will bring no personal gain. Generally, reversed Man signifies the individual's negative attitudes, expressed as pessimism, obstinacy, and an anti-social refusal to see other points of view. In relationships, reclusiveness and withdrawal are indicated. Spirituality, inverted Man signifies isolation from others of a like mind with whom one could otherwise progress.

Lagu

Old German, Laguz; Gothic, Lagus; Anglo-Saxon, Lagu; Old Norse, Lögr.

The Elder Futhark's 21st rune is Lagu. In all of the runic versions, it represents water in all of its flowing aspects. In the rune card painting, this rune is depicted as the leek plant, signifying the many roots of our existence which give us the basis for an upward growth in our passage through life. This path leads us in manifold ways up to the bend which leads us back to the place from which we have come; back down to the Mother Goddess, earth. The element of energy, the fire of life, cannot exist in isolation. It is integral with the air, water, and earth, each of which possess their own characteristic energy qualities, ranging from the softness of the breeze to the hardness of rock. The energy of water implicit in Lagu is expressed by the waterfall behind the leek. Here, the stream of energy of the cascade denotes impetuous energy and strength.

This rune's name is related to the French word *lac,* and the English words "lake" and "lagoon," all of which mean "enclosed water."

Primarily, however, Lagu is the rune of flow, symbolizing both the uncertainties and vast potential of existence. As flowing water, Lagu is the medium by which passage may be gained. But, as with all transitions and journeys, this passage is not without risk, so Lagu has a twofold character. Human beings cannot live without water, yet water can kill us by drowning. As noted in the Old English Rune Poem, "To land lovers, water seems annoying if they set forth on a rocking ship, they are terrified by the waves of the sea terrify them, and the horse of the sea pays no heed to its bridle." Appropriately, its deities are the ancient Earth Mother goddess Nerthus and the sea-god, Njord, and with the tide-generating influence of the lunar deity, Mani. Its element is, naturally, water; its specific polarity is female, as Lagu is the prime female rune (correspondingly, Tyr is the male).

In Lagu, the principle of appropriate balance is evident, for a dearth of something can be as destructive as an excess. Because of its fluxing nature, Lagu can signify any one of a number of polar opposites between which a proper balance is required for life and growth to exist and continue. That flow restores balance after a period of imbalance. The natural process of the Lagu principle was stated over 1,900 years ago by the pagan saint Appolonius of Tyana: "For things that violate Nature can hardly come to be: and in any case, even when they do come into existence, they pass rapidly to destruction." The natural balance of the world will, as a matter of course, re-assert itself again. Lagu expresses this truth. Lagu rules the period around May Day, the old Celtic summer's beginning festival of Beltane (April 29 to May 14). At Beltane, Lagu stands for the force of life and growth present in all matter, organic and inorganic. Lagu rules over wortcunning (herb lore), whose cultivational period is the summer half of the year which begins with Beltane. Lagu also signifies the cyclic progress of growth. It is present in the growth rings of trees and in shellfish. The leafy layers of the leek reflect this process of cyclic and concentric growth. In the human being, Lagu defines the female menstrual cycle. In its form of tidal waters, Lagu marks the ebb and flow of the tide. As the waterfall, it is the irresistible power of running water *en masse.*

Lagu is connected with energy change and growth, so it is a rune of magic, which can be defined as the control of energy change and growth in conformity with the will. The Old Norse word for sorcery is *lögr,* the rune's name in that tongue. Psychically, Lagu is a very important rune. It can be used in meditation to gain access to the unconscious mind, and in divination it will refer to the psychic elements of a question. Lagu is also connected linguistically with the word "law," being the law underlying the system of organic life and growth. The plant associated with the rune, the leek, is a plant of strong growth, whose phallic form indicates great potential energy.

In the Haindl Tarot, Lagu is allied with the trump XIV, Alchemy, equivalent to Temperance in other tarot decks. Here, Lagu can be taken as signifying the unity of matter, energy, and spirit through its many transformations. Here, spirit enters matter, and in turn, matter affects and is affected by the spirit. Within this transformation is the energy of flow and growth by which it is powered. The stream of mind flows from the past through the present and into the future. When it refers to a rite of passage, Lagu symbolizes the soul crossing the waters to the otherworld at death. In this aspect, Lagu is connected with the barque of the dead in the runes Kan and Bar.

When it turns upright in a divination, Lagu indicates that the querent's creative and imaginative faculties are well developed, and should be applied successfully. Lagu signifies that the tide of events has turned in the querent's favor, and he or she is capable now of taking on problems and defeating them, especially if there are other favorable runes in the spread such as Ur, Eiwaz, and Sig. Upright, this rune indicates that the querent will have a good memory, enabling her or him to profit from learning. It denotes growth through education, and the controlled exercise of a fertile imagination. More generally, one has been or is being offered the ability to flow with events. This can be the means to understand fashions and use them to one's profit, or it can indicate an aptitude for acting, the means to adapt to roles. To whatever aspect of life the question is addressed, the querent will be able to elicit the sympathy of others.

Spiritually, Lag indicates that the querent has considerable psychic abilities that can be used for the good. One's intuitive faculties are keen, and one should trust one's intuition in the matter under consideration. Any dream or premonition that the querent feels is relevant to the matter should be taken seriously. In spiritual terms, Lagu is sometimes called "the teacher's rune," for it signifies the inquirer's ability to receive spiritual teaching, and in turn pass it on coherently and wisely to those who can receive it well. In Anglo-Saxon England, this was the rune of leechdoms, wortcunning, and starcraft.

When the rune Lagu is written in its normal manner, with the "branch" to the right, it is the active form, signifying the flowing tide. In the other direction, the mirror image of Lagu, with the "branch" to the left, it signifies the ebbing of the tide. Combined, these two forms of the rune make the nineteenth rune, Ehwaz, the rune of combinations, partnerships, and emotional relationships. The shape of the rune Lagu is half that of the rune Ehwaz, which infers a flowing together of the two elements—active and passive—to create the whole.

Lagu inverted signifies loss of memory. One may overstretch one's resources, perhaps by taking on work which one is not equipped to do either through inexperience or over-confidence. This inversion warns the questioner that, although taking dangerous risks may seem to be an attractive option, it is certain to lead to disaster. One has the tendency to swim against the current of events, or to try to change everything except oneself. In matters of emotional relationships, Lagu inverted is taken to warn a man against becoming involved with a woman who will subject him to emotional control. When the querent is female, Lagu indicates fearfulness in a relationship, perhaps a dominant man with whom the woman has a relationship which she wishes, but fears, to end. Generally, in relationship terms, Lagu inverted denotes a lethargic, fearful personality subject to emotional blackmail by an unscrupulous partner. This leads, inevitably, to the futile pursuit of someone unattainable, and a series of failed love affairs. Also, when the question concerns one's own misdemeanors, Lagu inverted specifies that they will be found out, and retribution is inevitable. Spiritually, the inverted rune signifies that one may be getting "out of one's depth," into areas with which one is not yet equipped to deal. As with other matters, the inverted Lagu rune warns the querent that now is the time to get out of a bad situation before it is too late. In all questions, the warning of inverted Lagu is: don't wait, change the circumstances now!

ING

Old German, Ingwaz; Gothic, Iggws; Anglo-Saxon, Ing.

The 22nd rune is Ing, or Ingwaz. Hermann Haindl's card shows a brilliant, fiery rune floating amid darkness, like a square of heavenly light. This square or signifies the light of conformity with natural laws, and of fertility. Here, the secret of creation—conception and the generative power—is shown as a serpent gliding between smooth, warm stones. Like the Indian kundalini serpent, it will become erect soon in order to rise to a higher level.

In all versions of its name, this rune represents the fertility god, Ing, who is one aspect of the male consort of the Earth Mother goddess of fertility and nurturing, Nerthus. Ing is primarily a god of family and place, more specifically the god of the hearth fire, known in England and Scotland as the *ingle*. The Scots word for fuel is *inglin,* and a fireplace, sacred to Ing, is an *inglenook*. This rune has an especially protective quality for households, and is used widely in Britain as a sigil in brickwork. The rune is a symbol of light, firebrand, or beacon, transmitting a message far and wide. On an esoteric level, it is an astral doorway into other states of being. As Ingwaz or Yngvé, the god known as Ing is perceived as an aspect of Frey, whose ritual perambulations around his sacred enclosures in a consecrated wagon paralleled the ceremonies of Nerthus. The Old English Rune Poem records, "At first, Ing was seen by the eastern Danes, departing over the waves with his wagon. Thus the Heardings named this champion." Ing's sacred connections include the claim of the old kings of Sweden, the Ynglingar, to be descended from Yngvé-Frey. The peoples who lived around the shores of the North Sea were also his devotees or descendants. They were known as Ingvaeones, "The People of Ing." The famous 11th-century swordmaker, Ingelrii, whose weapons were much sought-after all over northern Europe, may have been a member of this fire-and-energy cult.

On a symbolic level, Ing stands for energy in a potential but as yet unreleased form (as in Inglin). The god Yngvé-Frey is the personification of the male generative power, the instigator of growth. One of the meanings of Ing is the male orgasmic force and its consequences. It is the potential energy accumulated gradually for a period before being released as a single burst of power. It is the potential of limitless extension reflected in the geometrical form of the rune itself. On a biological level, this rune has the form of the double helix of the DNA molecule, which is the basic means by which replication of organic cells occurs, reflecting the major meaning of the rune: process.

There are two basic forms of the rune Ing. One is an enclosed, continuous figure, while the other is clearly produced from the overlapping of two identical, but mutually inverted, figures. The latter version signifies the outgoing, yet completing, nature of this rune, a symbol of integration at all levels. Graphically, it symbolizes the law of the unity of opposites as applied to the year. At the Winter Solstice, the period of duration of light is at its most reduced, while darkness is at its maximum. As the Vernal Equinox approaches, the light increases, while the darkness decreases proportionally. At the equinox, the lines cross, with day and night divided equally. From that point onward, until the Summer Solstice, the light increases and the dark decreases proportionally. At the Summer Solstice, the center of the rune, the light is at its maximum and the darkness at its minimum. The process is then repeated once more in a mirror image of the previous sequence. The light declines and the darkness increases until the Autumnal Equinox, when they are equal once more. Then the increase and mutual decrease continue until the end of the rune, the Winter Solstice, is reached again. Thus the Ing rune contains within it a diagram of the relationship of darkness and light during the yearly cycle. It binds both qualities together in wholeness. In the runic year cycle, Ing rules the early summertime from May 14 until May 29.

Geometrically, the enclosed Ing rune is identical with the Egyptian Diamond of the English Freemasons' tradition. This figure is very important in the sacred geometry based upon the principles of Pythagoras. It is a symbol of wholeness, a mystic figure composed of four "Pythagorean triangles" arranged back-to-back. The hypotenuses of these four right-angled triangles of three, four, and five units make each of the sides of this "diamond" five units long. The "diamond" itself is eight units long and six units wide, having an area of 24 square units, relating it to the 24 runes of the Elder Futhark, of which it is a symbol.

Ing is a very good rune, signifying the satisfactory completion of one stage and pregressing to a better one. It may also signify that optimistic state of relief or release which accompanies the successful completion of a project. This may be the realization of a life-long ambition. In any case, activities involving integration, cooperation, and unification are favored, including the duties of being a parent. Spiritually, it signifies a transition from one state to the next. Generally, there is the possibility of an important, perhaps life-changing (but beneficial) event occurring. In any case, it indicates that the querent may soon be free from worries.

Ing's polarity is both masculine and feminine, and it is ruled by the elements of water and earth. It is the eighth of the nine non-invertible runes, so in runic readings using stones or letter cards, one will find no difference. However, in our cards, we can still see an inversion, which, as before, may indicate some lessening of the qualities inherent in the rune. Reversed, it will have the meaning of a less fortunate outcome to the project or event than the querent would ideally like, though it by no means indicates failure. As in all things, there can be either a beneficial or unfortunate termination of events, and when the card is inverted, then a less favorable interpretation must be made. It indicates a slowing down of progress, a more difficult process in general. Changes may be not for the better, at least not in the short term. Completion of projects may not occur as satisfactorily as one might hope them to, bringing new worries. But these problems are not likely to be serious, merely nuisances.

OÐAL

Old German, Othila; Gothic, Othal; Anglo-Saxon, Ethel.

The 23rd stave of the Elder Futhark is Odal. The corresponding rune card shows Odal as two gnarled tree stumps, that touch each other with their pointed ends. This is reminiscent of the "heavenly touch" by the fingertips (as depicted in the painting by Michelangelo in the Sistine Chapel at the Vatican in Rome), where the divine power is transferred from the heavenly to the earthly world. In touching, the stumps form a square standing on its corner, as in the rune Ing. It is an enclosure for the heavenly light that shines forth to be mirrored in a brook springing from the moorland. This brook also mirrors the patch of blue sky above, emphasizing the ancient Hermetic maxim, "as above, so below."

The Odal rune signifies the homestead. In Old German, its name means "ancestral property;" in Gothic, "property;" and in Anglo-Saxon, "property" or "homeland." In traditional society, it signifies the irremovable ancestral property of the family and the land which goes with it. In the language of Frisia, this rune is called *Eeven-eerde,* which means "own earth" or "own land." This is a perfect expression of the qualities present in this rune. Odal is described by the Old English Rune Poem thus: "Home loved by all human beings, if there they can peacefully prosper and enjoy frequent harvests." Odal symbolizes that enclosure with which it is necessary to surround any possession. Symbolically, the rune signifies the belonging, togetherness, inheritance, and also the non-material qualities which must be handed on from generation to generation. When it refers to possessions, these are the sorts of possessions which cannot moved around: houses and land, intellectual property, or spiritual possessions.

Odal signifies innate qualities and material and spiritual heritage. These qualities are ascribed especially to the protection of Odin. But it need not just mean one's own dwelling or possessions, physical or conceptual. It has the meaning also of one's place, perhaps in society, or more generally in the scheme of things. Magically, the rune Odal is a resistance against the arbitrary intrusion into personal life of the rule of human government. Odal signifies the individual's integrity and human rights, protected through careful and thoughtful management of resources. It represents the liberty of the individual, the family, and the clan within the overall framework of natural justice.

When the Odal rune is upright in a runecast, it is beneficial. Odal denotes safety and protection in all matters. It signifies fortunate results to questions concerning domestic property, family interests, and social life. Where financial matters are concerned, Odal represents money that is not immediately available, such as inheritances and bequests which have not yet been realized; or other inaccessible money, such as in a pension fund or money in trust. But when it falls in association with other "wealth" runes, such as Feo, Jera, and Bar, Odal denotes materialism, to the detriment of the spiritual aspects of life. An addiction to consumerism and a love of fashion in all its forms is indicated here, but this may be rationalized as an improvement of the family's lifestyle rather than the individual's. Spiritually, Odal represents the individual's reception of ancestral tradition, the spiritual skills and wisdom of former generations of one's family and ethnic background. All of us, from whatever background we come, have our own "spiritual roots," and Odal instructs us to take heed of them, for they are part of our örlog.

Inverted, Odal signifies delay, exclusion, and the accompanying loss. Even when success appears to be imminent, something may happen to delay it for a considerable period. Too-rapid progress will lead to over-stretching resources, and consequent failure of the enterprise. There is also the likelihood of loss in a project through one's slovenliness or lack of attention to detail. But whatever damage is done to one's chances is as the result of one's own lack of perception. Where the question involves travel, problems are indicated, possibly an accident. The common feature connecting these potential disasters is the individual whose own actions have led to these results.

Odal inverted can also specify a problem that money or inherited position cannot solve. Here, legal action will do no good, even if the subject appears to be in the right. If the question concerns legal matters, problems with a will or other form of inheritance are indicated. One may be involved in a dispute over the ownership of a piece of land, access rights, or other common disputes that arise between neighbors. In financial terms, it may involve the unexpectedly early calling-in of a loan, repossession, or the seizure of property by legal authorities. When the question refers to the individual's relationships, parents and relatives disapprove. Reversed Odal may also indicate a marriage against the expressed wishes of the family. Whatever the consequences of this action, the querent must be conscious of them, and take them without complaint if they are problematic. More generally, even if he or she is unaccustomed to doing so, the querent will be compelled to be self-reliant, depending on no one for assistance. The problem must be solved by the individual's will and capability alone. There is no one else to blame if things go wrong.

ᛞᚪᚷ

Old German, Dagaz; Gothic, Dags; Anglo-Saxon, Dæg.

The 24th and last rune of the Elder Futhark is Dag, or Dagaz. The runic card of Dag depicts the wholeness of a complete day: the light and the dark. In the human being, this symbolizes the conscious and the unconscious parts of the mind. In the light of day, colors are vivid, and objects are sharply defined. In the darkness, everything is gray, colorless. Only the fire of night contains all colors, yet it also sometimes brings fear, as it seems more potent than it does by day. As the fire of the hearth, however, it also brings warmth and security. Symbolically, the day signifies the exoteric nature of things, and the night, the esoteric side. This homogeneity is in accordance with the principle of holistic unity that underlies all existence.

The rune name "Dag" specifies day in all of its linguistic variants. Dag's meaning is expressed beautifully in the Old English Rune Poem: "Day is the gods' messenger, the light means happiness and consolation to rich and poor alike." As day, Dag is also the rune that rules midday, midsummer, and the principles of opening and sudden change. In the runic time cycle, Dag covers the lightest period of the year, from June 14 until June 29, with the Summer Solstice at its mid-point. It is the rune of light as the source of strength and well-being.

Dag is one of the most beneficial runes, signifying light, health, prosperity, and openings of all kinds. In the runic time cycle, Dag represents the high point of the year. Although this may appear to be the apotheosis of light, this time is also the beginning of the decline. Dag thus marks the point conjunction, that time and place where seeming opposites are unified. Dag is therefore a rune of catalysis. It causes or marks sudden change, without being changed itself. This is the class of events studied by catastrophe theory, which is where something apparently in a stable state suddenly "topples over" into another, quite different, yet also stable, state. This concept, expressed scientifically relatively recently, was known to ancient rune-masters. In East Anglian and Scots dialects of English, a *dag* describes a sudden downpour of rain, an immediate transition from a dry to a wet state.

Esoterically, Dag signifies the state of cosmic consciousness. In its geometrical form, the Dag rune expresses the necessary balance between the polarities, especially light and darkness. It signifies the "law of the unity of opposites," and may be considered the Northern Tradition version of the Chinese yin and yang sigil. It is that which Edred Thorsson calls "the ódhinic paradox," the mystical moment that contains within it the seeming opposites of existence. This is expressed in the "law of the unity of opposites," which concerns itself with those things which modern western thought perceives as sepa-rate (the fragmental-opposite theory of existence), but which, in the polar-complete (holistic) view of the universe of the Northern Tradition, are not separate at all, but aspects of the greater whole.

As well as symbolizing the unity of day and night, Dag reflects the cycles of the seasons. Dag is the rune of midday and the Summer Solstice, which at once is the high point of the sun's light and the commencement of its decline toward darkness and winter. Dag rules the half-month starting on June 14 and ending on June 29. At opposite sides of the year cycle, the runes Dag and Jera are also opposite forms to one another. Dag, at midday and midsummer, is an outgoing rune, while Jera, located at midnight and midwinter, is an ingathering one. Dag is also the runic equivalent to Duir (Derna, the oak tree) in the Celtic Ogham tree alphabet. As with the Dag rune, Duir rules the period of midsummer, the oaken door linking the rising half of the year with the declining half. Magically, Dag is the rune of invisibility, that perfect integration with the background which renders something or someone unnoticed. In modern terms, it is the rune of camouflage. As a rune of protection, its form is used as a prophylactic sigil on doorposts. When painted on a doorpost, its customary colors are white and blue, or white and green. The elements corresponding with Dag are fire and air, and its ruling divinity is the watcher-god, Heimdall.

Dag is the ninth and final non-invertible rune. But, as with the other non-invertible runes, as a card there is a reversed meaning. This card represents the skies of day and night, expressing their essential unity. The boundaries of twilight, evening and morning, are divined by the double-triangle shape of the rune. Transition zones such as twilight are the boundaries at which the veil between this world and the otherworld are thin. Dag is a supremely beneficial rune, along with Kan and Sig, as a rune of the solar power. This power ensures success against obstacles to progress; the demolition of barriers and the will to carry a project through to a successful conclusion. Generally, it denotes a self-motivated, positive attitude which is necessary for success.

When a decision is needed, Dag indicates that the querent will find new insights into the matter. It signifies that a change of mind or an adjustment of attitude may be necessary for success. Where a sudden change is indicated, it is a change for the better. When the other cards with Dag are less favorable, it specifies that the inquirer has a negative attitude toward the situation rather than the situation itself being unfavorable. The only negative aspects in the reading are those coming from inside the individual, not from the environment. One should alter one's attitude toward one's circumstances, and then matters will improve.

Upright with less beneficial runes, Dag can mitigate their influence, indicating a good outcome despite them. Binding runes, such as Not and Is, which threaten delay or hindrance, are minimized, and inverted runes are altered from their bad implications into nothing more than delayers. Of course, like Sig, Dag actually enhances the qualities of good runes with which it may appear. It will enhance the reading ascribed to the runes associated with growth and increase, such as Feo, Bar, and Lagu. When Dag is upright, it may signify the light of dawn which comes after darkness. Inverted, it signifies the opposite—darkness that comes after light.

YR

Anglo-Saxon and Old Norse, Yr.

Yr is the 25th rune in our runic system. Hermann Haindl's painting depicts Yr as the three roots of the ancient, gnarled World Tree, reaching down into the soil of the earth and into the waters of inspiration. It is a starry night, with a waning moon. The tree's trunk spirals upward in a clockwise direction, linking the lower with the upper; as if in opposition, an ivy creeper spirals around and down the tree's trunk like a serpent. The upper part of the tree is forked like Kan. Within the upper fork shines the morning star. This upper forked trunk links with the lower triadic root that represents the principle of Yr itself. The whole form of the tree is that of Yrmingsul or Ermings-säule-Irminsul, the cosmic axis. Below, the waters reflect both the star and the tree. As it stretches upward toward Asgard, its reflection goes ever downward into the underworld, expressing the maxim, "as above, so below." In the background, we see the reverse side of the Externsteine, the central sanctuary of the Teutonic Elder Faith. In front, a pierced, squared-off rock stands like a natural altar.

Yr is a rune which is not present in the Elder Futhark of mainland Europe, but which was added to the rune-row by the Anglo-Saxon in England. Subsequently, it became the magical ending-rune in the Norse sixteen-character Futhark. In both Anglo-Saxon and Old Norse, the rune Yr means "the bow made of yew wood." In those days, the best longbows were made from the wood of the yew tree. In ancient times, the bow was a formidable weapon whose construction and use required considerable skill. According to The Old English Rune Poem, "The Bow is a joy to Æthelings and Earls, an indication of worth, looking good on a steed, rapid in its course, an excellent weapon." Here, Yr's bow reflects the combination of physical and mental skills necessary for achievement. But in addition to being the most deadly long-range weapon in the days before firearms, the bow was also used in geomancy. An appropriate place, chosen by Ullr, the god of bows, could be located by the fall of an arrow. Customarily, a hero on his deathbed would shoot a final arrow to divine the location of his grave. In English legend, this method was employed by the outlaws Robin Hood and Little John, and the giant warrior Piers Shonkes.

This rune is related closely to Eihwaz; both are sacred to the yew tree. Yr, however, is active magically, while Eihwaz is more passive in its function. The rune tree in this card has the three roots of Yggdrassil. In Norse tradition, the world-tree or cosmic axis is an ash tree. But some authorities, such as Edred Thorson, think that this cosmic ash was not meant to be an actual broad-leafed ash tree, but a yew. This is plausible, as Yggdrassil is said to be evergreen, and a by-name of the yew tree in Old Norse is *barraskr* (needle ash). An alternative interpretation of the name Yggdrassil is "yew-column." This world tree is known sometimes as Mjótvidhr, "The Tree of Measure," a central point in relation to which all other things may be related. In the Northern Tradition, there are two serpents which coil around the world tree: Niodhoggr, which twines around the root and trunk, gnawing away at it and threatening its stability; and

Jörmungand, the serpent that lies in the ocean at the edge of the world. Both of these are aspects of the vouivre, the dragon-like personification of the önd within the Earth. As the central point, Yr has no place in the runic time cycle of the year. It encompasses all time and no time. Although the Jörmungand, has her own rune in the Anglo-Saxon and Northumbrian rune-rows, she is covered by the Yr card in this system.

The Tree of Measure has three roots, each of which lie in a different realm: Niflheim, Midgard, and Asgard. Beneath each of the three roots of Yggdrassil lies a mystic spring or well. The root in Niflheim grows over the spring of Hvergelmir, literally, "the seeing cauldron," from whence comes the destructive, corpse-chewing worm, Niodhoggr. In Midgard, Mimir's Well lies beneath its corresponding root. This is literally "The Headwater of Memory," into which Odin cast one of his eyes for a draught of enlightenment. Odin's eye, symbolic of the Full Moon, lies in this well, sometimes accompanied by Heimdall's horn, Gjällarhorn, whose curved form echoes the crescent phases of the Moon. The third root of Yggr's steed overlies the Urdar Fountain, where the three Norns spin people's Wyrds. In the pool of this spring swim two swans, the plumage of which is used by the Norns when they travel the earth to spy on human activities. The needle ash Yggrdrassil thus links the three cosmic planes of the lower, middle, and upper worlds: Asgard, Midgard, and Utgard. This three-fold cosmic axis is a major spiritual concept in the Northern Tradition, present both in the Germanic-Norse and the Celtic versions of the tradition. In the Celtic version, the upper world is Gwynvyd, the White Land; the middle world, Abred; and the lower world, Annwn, the abyss. The cosmic axis is the means by which souls and the spiritually enlightened may travel between these states of being.

As Yggdrassil, the tree is also the gallows, literally Yggr's Steed (Yggr is one of Odin's many by-names), referring to the tree upon which he hung for nine days and nine nights to obtain runes for humankind. An Old Norse poetic kenning for the gallows is "the horse of the hanged." In the Old English Rune Poem, there is the oblique reference of the "steed" under this rubric. This tradition of the triple-rooted cosmic axial tree as gallows was continued in London until as late as the eighteenth century. There, it was manifest as the notorious ancient scaffold at Tyburn, the triangular Triple Tree, which was a gallows with three uprights, and therefore three posts (or "roots") in the ground. It stood at an important crossways, like all crossroads, symbolic of the center of the world. The power of the triangle was present there to ward off the harmful thoughts and curses of the executed. The herbs ascribed to Yr, the bryony and the mandrake, are those which traditionally grew beneath the gallows, and from which alrauns are fashioned.

The rune Yr is sacred to Odin, Frigg, and Vidar, who symbolize all of the elements together, and is both female and male in polarity. It is connected with the tarot trump XVI, The Tower. This trump signifies the descent of the life force from above, and its linking with the chthonic forces of the waters in the Earth. The materialistic view of human life is overthrown, and the spiritual takes its rightful place in society. Here, Yr signifies spiritual truth, destruction of false creeds, and unsound reasoning.

Around the 1960s, the so-called "blank rune" was introduced by American rune masters. In *The Book of Runes,* Ralph Blum calls this "the Unknowable." More commonly, this so-called "blank rune" is called Wyrd by some rune-users, as though the force of Wyrd were not acting through any rune reading already! The reason for this invention, it appears, was so that an additional element of randomness should be brought into runecasts. This was rather woolly thinking, however, to insert a new, confusing factor into what was, before that, a precise oracle. Any random, meaningless element must tend to make things less clear, and this is especially true with the runes.

The nature of this so-called "rune" seems to be allied to another American invention, the "wild card" in the playing card deck. This wild card, or Joker, was introduced in New York in the 1850s and led to the development of new card games like Euchre. This randomizing process continued in the early part of this century, when the casino owners at Monte Carlo, wishing to increase the odds in favor of the bank, introduced first the zero and then the double zero into roulette.

Some runecasters make the blank rune represent the inevitable, that which cannot be avoided. Often this is interpreted as meaning "fate" in a fatalistic sense; something predestined, already determined, like the next page of this book. This idea of a fixed, predetermined future is not part of the spiritual roots of the runes in the Northern Tradition. It denies the free will of the individual, something upon which the fundamental pagan ideas of individual freedom, freedom of conscience, and accountability for one's actions are based. If "Wyrd" is taken to mean "fatal predestination," then it has no place in runecasting. Because of this, we have chosen to use the Anglo-Saxon and Norse rune, Yr, as a 25th in place of a blank rune. Of course, as with all things, the rune Yr is part of wYRd! The real rune enables the querent to use both standard divinations using 24 runes, and also readings which require 25, designed originally for the "blank rune." Readers who object to using a 25th rune may remove this card from the deck when doing divinations and use it as a ruler, significator, or meditational card.

This rune is the final invertible stave. Like the other invertibles, Yr can express two meanings. Upright, it relates to defense, protection against unseen attack, and the ability to determine the correct location in which to conduct one's affairs. The defensive indications of this rune denote that rivals should fail decisively in their attempt to subvert one's efforts. Any project which the inquirer might be contemplating should be well supported with strong foundations, ensuring its continuity over a long period. Generally, steadiness in all matters is signified by Yr in the upright position, originating in inspiration that the subject has the ability to apply in a practical way. In business, Yr signifies that even when others might fail, the questioner will remain solvent. One has the power of endurance, both personally and in corporate terms. But the undertaking in question should not be totally materialistic in its aims. It should have at least some charitable and socially responsible elements. Spiritually, the subject is centered. He or she is in the enviable position of being in the right place at the right time. From this, spiritual creativity can flow.

Yr in a runecast signifies success when referring to professions involving surveying, navigation, biological architecture, and others requiring geolocational qualities. This sense of location may also refer to the good location of the querent's dwelling or business premises.

When inverted, Yr does not have the same meaning as Eiwaz, the rune it now resembles. It is simply an inversion of Yr, which signifies disruption of order and the inversion of the qualities discussed above. When it is reversed, Yr indicates that the querent is subject to attack. One may be under attack from many directions at once. Rivals can take advantage of the subject's weak points, which are emphasized at this time. One is likely to make serious misjudgments, and one's attempts in achieving objectives will be badly off-target. There may be a general failure of inspiration, and the individual will feel out of place. He or she is not centered, either physically or spiritually. Reversed, Yr defines a lack of endurance or continuity, disruption of the querent's plans, and generally a chaotic life.

THE VALKNUT

The shape of the rune pictures and the pattern on the reverse of Hermann Haindl's rune cards is the equilateral hexagon. This shape is derived from the Hagal rune, whose meaning of formative causation is expressed through the hexagonal lattice structure of matter. The pattern on the back of the rune cards is composed of a series of six Valknuts within the overall hexagonal pattern.

The Valknut is an ancient Anglo-Saxon and Norse sigil composed of three interlinked equilateral triangles. Its name means "the knot of the chosen ones." Sometimes the Valknut is depicted with an eye at the center, denoting the single, yet all-seeing, eye of the Allfather, Odin. The Valknut is made up of three interlaced triangles. In this ingenious form, each of the three colored triangles comes into contact with the other two colors in three ways: as the outer, inner, and middle rows of the figure. The Valknut is, par excellence, a figure of integration of three identical, yet separate, patterns or qualities. In general, these three triangles represent the triadic nature of existence. They can stand for the three states of time: past, present, and future, expressed as the three Norns: Urd, Verdandi, and Skuld. They also represent the three planes of existence: the underworld, Annwn; the middleworld, Abred; and the upperworld, Gwynvyd. Similarly, the three triangles signify the traditional three states of the human being: body, spirit, and soul. The colors of the Valknut represent the main colors of Bifröst, the rainbow bridge that links the earth with the heaven. Each Valknut figure is composed of nine lines, which symbolize the nine worlds of Norse cosmology, and the "power of three times three."

Overall, the Valknut invokes the power of the essential, eternal unity of space and time. On the rune card, six Valknuts are brought together in hexagonal form. In all, these six Valknuts are composed of nineteen triangles, which represent the eighteen Lays of Power described in the ancient Norse scripture, Hávamál, upon which Guido von List based the Armanen system of runes using eighteen staves. In Northern Tradition spirituality, the number eighteen is very important: the eighteenth rune is an ancient kenning for a "great mystery" that is contained in life itself.

PART III
DIVINATION AND ITS
TECHNIQUES

"The present is the daughter of the past, and the mother of the future."

This ancient adage underlies all existence, that being our presence within time. This presence is understood usually in a tripartite way, the present being perceived as the middle link between the past and the future. In a mythic form, the Three Fates and the Norns are personifications of this triadic perception of the three parts of time. But these three parts of time are not equivalent to one another. The past is fixed, and cannot be changed. It is known, or at least partially recorded. The present is in constant flux. It is being experienced now, and is apparent, even if our perception of it is imprecise. But the future, which has not happened yet, is totally unknown; ever since the rise of human consciousness, this has been a main human preoccupation.

Since the earliest part of recorded history, and doubtless before that, people have made attempts to glimpse visions of the future. The concept that this was possible at all seems to have come first from the world of dreams. In dreams, people have visited places long since destroyed, or places which do not exist in the material world; they have talked with the dead, they have had visions of events which, later, appear to have occurred in reality. In the deleria of illness, through near-death experiences, and by hallucinations brought about by disease, injury, or drugs, humans have unwittingly and sometimes unwillingly contacted areas of experience that are closed to the waking consciousness of everyday life. Through these experiences, albeit in the inner space of the mind, real and valuable knowledge has been gained. Because of this, the shamans of every culture have entered voluntarily into this dangerous uncharted terrain: they have climbed alone onto almost airless mountain tops; gone into trances mimicking death; ingested dangerous, sometimes toxic substances; fasted; and performed ceremonial rites of self-injury, willingly undergoing ordeals at the edge of death. In so doing they have experienced dreams, hallucinations, and visions of other states of being. Those returning to some level of sanity after such experiences have brought back with them descriptions of other worlds—including that of the future.

Historically, divination appears to have developed out of shamanism, where the direct experience of shamans and oracles was eventually replaced by readings taken from a variety of sources. At first, divination seems to have been a very specialized art. In a highly-skilled technique, diviners examined the entrails of sacrificed animals in attempts to predict the future. Gradually, though, the omens read by professional diviners, who were usually priests, became routine and formalized. This gave some degree of uniformity in readings, and also made the job of the diviner easier. Rules were developed in which certain abnormalities signified corresponding predictions. For teaching purposes, the entrails of sacrificed animals, examined in this art of hepatoscopy, were modeled in clay and bronze, and eventually these patterns replaced the real thing. Apart from being cheaper than sacrificing an animal every time a divination was required, these formalized systems were more convenient, more rapid, and easier to interpret. From this period of formalization, many sorts of divination developed, some of which are practiced still today.

In former times, people resorted to various techniques of "fortune telling" that gave positive results in terms of shapes, images, or symbols which could be interpreted more readily than sometimes vague psychic impressions. When thrown, the Astragali, the tarsal-bones of sheep, can fall in four distinct ways. Because of this, they were used as a divinatory oracle in ancient Babylon and Greece, where various "casts" had their corresponding meanings. Astragali were the forerunner of dice, which were used in divination long before they became the gambler's bane. The forms of divination which have come down to us from antiquity are myriad: they include divination by many different methods. The most fundamental types of divination are based upon the phenomena of natural forces. Taking the traditional four elements, these are pyromancy, which uses fire; aeromancy, which studies the winds and clouds; hydromancy, studying water in its various forms; and geomancy, divination by and on the earth. Among other forms of divination, practitioners have also used oneiromancy, which is divination by dreams; rhabdomancy, by the divining rod; cereoscopy, by wax-shapes; crithomancy, by bread or cakes; coscinoscopy, by sieve; kleidoscopy, by key; and crystallomancy, by gazing into a crystal ball. But the most formalized of divination systems, those using specific symbols, are the most popular today; these include tarot cards and the runes.

A vital factor in our approach to divination is our perception of what the words "the future" actually mean. Belief in predestination, that everything that happens has already been worked out and is merely being operated now, has often been used as a basis for claims of divination's effectiveness. In this view, divination lets us see a few pages ahead in the book of existence. Those pages already exist in some way, and using the right methods can enable us to read them. This is the doctrine of fatalism. To the fatalist, the future already exists and is immutable. We are literally "fated."

The narrative style of filmmaking, developed in Hollywood in the early part of this century, unconsciously promotes a certain view of events which tends to enforce the doctrine of fatalism. We have all seen the sort of intercut sequences that show a vehicle speeding from the right and another speeding from the left—cut to vehicle speeding from the left—cut to vehicle speeding from the right—then to the left one, a little further along the road—then to the right one, and so on, until finally a head-on collision between the two vehicles is shown. We tend to view this cinematic representation as a true depiction of the reality of such an "event." But in the real world, this is a distortion of reality. The events "leading up" to the accident only have a reality in relation to the accident when recounted after the fatal event has taken place. In the film, the two vehicles were going to collide. This was because the writer and director arranged it so, and showed this formative process of the accident in an obvious, theatrical manner. But in reality, although there is a statistical chance that the vehicles might collide, the only time that it is actually inevitable is at the point when all avoiding actions are impossible. Before that, any number of other actions and reactions are possible, and no collision, or even the hint of the possibility of a collision, would occur.

In the film, the portrayal of the accident has already been filmed and edited to portray a fictional event before it is witnessed by the spectator. When the film is shown, it is in reality nothing more than an edited record of fiction enacted in the past. The "events" one witnesses are already there in sequential images, fixed and immutable. But in reality there is only a possibility that something might happen. Even when something does happen, say the vehicular accident, we can only speak of something happening "before the accident" in a historical sense. For most predicted events, we cannot even use the phrase "before it happens," because there is no certainty that it will take place at all. Only in the fatalistic view of the world, where our lives are unfolding like a movie, can there be certainty of this kind. And this view involves a serious paradox, too. Fatalism makes divination a pointless exercise, for if we have no free will on our actions, then divination must have been pre-programmed into the "cosmic film-show" along with everything else. Such a paranoid view of the world would make life nothing but an empty, mechanical performance, a play being performed by unknowing performers for the benefit, presumably, of sadistic extra-human onlookers.

A diametrically opposite world view is that the future is completely random and therefore totally unknowable. People who hold this viewpoint often see divination merely in terms of gambling, such as the "predictions" of the winners in horse races or the results of football matches. Outside of exceptional circumstances, however, divination is not about that kind of prediction. It is more like saying "a horse will win the race," the recognition that, if all of the processes leading up to the staging and running of the horse race come to fruition, then the race will take place and there will be a winner. If, however, some other factor intervenes, and the race is canceled, then there will not be a winner.

Most practitioners of divination do not hold either the fatalistic or the negativistic view of the future. They know that in some way, the technique of divination can give the inquirer a relevant report of the state of the universe at the time that the divination is made. From this report, tendencies and trends of events can be discerned. Whether or not the inquirer will gain useful results from the divination depends on the successful recognition of these trends of current events. These are the processes, which, if they continue in the same way as they are proceeding at present, will lead inevitably to certain results. Weather forecasters use exactly this technique. They examine the weather at the present moment, in relation to their records of what has gone before. They take into account the known facts of the climate, the season, and weather patterns in other areas which influence the area in question. The processes of weather-movement, known from observation of previous weather systems, are evaluated, and a forecast is made. Of course, the forecasters are not always 100% successful in their predictions. Random events, unforeseen factors, insufficient data, and human error all add to the failure rate. But, in general, weather forecasting is successful. Many people who decry the possibility of meaningful divination accept weather forecasting because it has a scientific basis. It is grounded on scientific observation and knowledge of the physical processes involved in weather-patterns.

Divination works according to exactly the same principles. The interpretation of the patterns presented to us in divination is achieved by taking into account our knowledge of what has happened in the past, recognizing the patterns within our own experience, and judging the likely result of the continuation of these trends. Divination gives us information of present trends and processes which are in our power to alter by our own conscious actions. It gives us a view of what is liable to happen if we do not do anything to alter the process. Free will means that, in most cases, we can turn aside from the course which is indicated by the result of the divination. Far from just informing us of our impending doom in a fixed, fatalistic future, divination can give us a means to avoid problems, and to live a better, more harmonious life. Although many people have debased divination into a side-show or a televised spectacle, it is still a serious business.

Unfortunately, divination is often conducted under the wrong conditions, by the wrong person, and at the wrong time because the practitioner does not know what the right conditions are. When this happens, it is scarcely likely that significant results will be obtained. Traditional writers on divination have always stressed the importance of practicing divination under the appropriate conditions. For example, both the medieval writer Gerardus Cremonensis (1114-1187) and the renaissance magician Heinrich Cornelius Agrippa (1468-1535) both warned against undertaking divination in the wrong frame of mind or when inappropriate conditions are prevailing. "You must always take heed," wrote Gerardus Cremonensis, "that you do not ask a question in very rainy, cloudy, or very windy weather, or when you are angry, or when the mind is busied with many affairs; nor with tempters or deriders, neither should you recast and reiterate the same question once again under the same figure or form; for this is error."

The prerequisite of doing a divination, then, is for the practitioner to get into the proper frame of mind. Being disturbed by anger, worries, or other preoccupations is almost certain to lead to error. But the prevailing weather conditions also affect one's performance markedly. Although today we might use technical words like "low pressure" or "cyclone" to describe these weather conditions, they are still inappropriate circumstances for diviners. Finally, the presence of those people called "negative influences," or as Gerardus Cremonensis dubbed them, "tempters or deriders," may lead to failure. It has been noted that such "negative influences" can prevent the proper functioning of direct divinations, such as those of water diviners. A similar effect on runic divinations can be expected.

Plain physical conditions may affect a divination adversely, too. A house or room close to high-voltage power lines is inappropriate, as is one where disruption from traffic noise is apparent. The reason for taking such precautions is that the runecaster's intuitive faculties necessary for divination will be suppressed under certain weather, physical, or mental conditions. Also, if the diviner performs a runic reading in a frivolous or uninterested manner, then he or she runs the risk of blunting those intuitive qualities required of a runecaster. Repeatedly reading at the wrong time or under the wrong conditions may even permanently reduce one's ability for runecasting.

It is also important not to perform divinations to ascertain each and every trivial aspect of life. The runes, or indeed any form of divination, should be an indication to free people of their possible actions in circumstances where the way ahead is not clear. Historically, divination became a crutch for some people, who have been reported subsequently by critics of divination as examples of "gross superstition." According to contemporary accounts, for example, in the mid-19th century Queen Ránaválona I of Madagascar would not take any action without first having a geomantic divination done to determine whether or not it was auspicious to go ahead. This included such matters as getting out of bed in the morning, or whether she should receive a visitor. Clearly, her life was blighted by an over-reliance on divination. Today, we read occasionally of film stars and business people who are alleged to base their whole lives upon the advice of either their astrologers, tarot or I Ching readers. The user of any powerful divination techniques can become over-reliant upon them—a "prediction addict." The runes, like anything else in human culture, exist to serve and guide us. They should never become our rulers, our substitutes for conscious free will.

USING THE RUNES

There are many ways of using the runes in divination. Some people will simply want to pull one card from the pack to get an "instant reading." Others will take note of the runecaster's position and the direction in which the divination is made before conducting a full ceremonial runecasting. Whichever method one chooses, the rune user should do the divination with reverence, in an appropriate frame of mind.

One important ceremonial technique of rune-reading is known as *ræd wæn,* "riding the wagon," where the runecaster can be placed metaphorically in the position of the god or goddess on the wagon, from which all things can be seen. "Riding the wagon" is a ceremonial act in which the actual casting, the shoat, or shoot, can be performed.

When it is carried out ceremonially, runecasting must take the surrounding physical and psychic environment into account. When it is to be conducted indoors, the main axis of the room—the right line—is the guiding principle. This is a imaginary line across the floor which can be determined readily. Theoretically, this line should be the alignment which is best in harmony with the energies of the earth in that room. In a building where the walls are oriented correctly, that is, facing the four cardinal directions, the axis should be east-west. In the Northern Tradition, this is the non-adversarial direction, at right angles to the presence of the gods in the north. (The adversarial orientation has the "plaintiff" facing northwards to be judged by the judge, who faces southwards at the "presence" in the north.) If that is not possible, it should lie parallel to the longer wall, dividing the floor space into two parts.

The location of the shoat itself is along this axial right line. The area is a white cloth whose dimensions are defined by the bodily dimensions of the runecaster. This is the runecaster's own length from his or her feet to the fingertips, held at full stretch above the head. Its width is the distance between the runecaster's outstretched arms, measured from fingertip to fingertip. The cloth is placed on the floor in such a way that its central point is located one-third of the way along the right line. The view of the runecaster is thus along the longer part of the room. The wall in front of the runecaster is considered positive, and the wall behind, negative. Proper orientation means that east is positive, and west is negative, with the presence north to the left and south to the right. As viewed by the inquirer, the direction along the right line toward the positive wall is considered "up," and that nearer to the runecaster, "down." "Left" and "right" refer to the caster's left and right.

Out of doors, this right line should face the position of the sun at the time that the divination is taking place. According to custom, the direction of human energy flow is toward the sun, in return for the sun's energy coming toward the world of humans. Of course, this direction depends on the time of day. At true midday, the sun stands due south, and at midnight (though invisible "beneath the earth"), it is due north. Other times of day and night have their own orientation, the sun appearing to compete a whole cycle in 24 hours. Each of these 24 hours corresponds with one of the 24 runes of the Elder Futhark. The whole circle of runes can be visualized as if one were standing inside a circular building with a series of stained glass windows all round, with each rune in its appropriate position, occupying 1/24 of the circle. Then, one would be able to see each rune illuminated in turn at the correct hour, because each rune corresponds with a compass direction that is also the direction of the sun at a certain hour of the 24-hour cycle. Jera stands in the north, with Dag in the south. The rune of the east is Bar, and that of the west, Kan. The other runes fit in the correct order into their corresponding "slots" in the circle.

The duration of each runic hour is from the "half" before the "hour" until the "half" after it. Thus, using the 24-hour clock, the runic hour of Jera runs from 23.30 hours until 00.30 hours. The next runic hour, Eoh, runs from 00.30 until 1.30; Peorth from 1.30 to 2.30, and so on. The final runic hour in the circle, ruled by Dag, runs from 11.30 until 12.30 hours. The beginning of the cycle with Feo commences at 12.30 running until 13.30, when the rune for the next hour is Ur. Using local solar time, the sun is in any one runic direction at the corresponding time of day. In general, runic divinations should not be conducted during the hours of darkness. According to tradition, such procedures should take place "In the face of the sun, and the eye of the light." But runecasts carried out for special reasons in relation to the runic directions may have to be performed at night, because they may be conducted in the direction of a specific rune, and at the runic hour. Then the right line that one uses must face toward the apparent position of the sun, whether it is visible or not.

Whatever the location and circumstances of the divination, the runecaster should sit on a cushion at the negative end. The cushion might be a ceremonial object embroidered with appropriate sigils, known as the *stol*. At the positive end of the white cloth, upon another special cloth, is located a personal talisman, the *mearomot*. This mearomot can be a medicine-bag, a special stone, crystal, raven's feather, or any other object which can assist the concentration of the runecaster. Whatever it is, it should embody something of the essence of the person. The paper bearing the question should accompany the talisman. Symbolic objects should be located at the four corners of the shoat also. When the ceremonial arrangement is complete, the runecaster should perform his or her mental cleansing and ceremonies, and then the question should be asked.

The querent should think hard about the question before it is formulated. It should be straightforward, and not couched in ambiguous language. It should refer to one concept only, and avoid muddled thought. The runes cannot give an intelligible answer if the question is not reasonable in the first place. The question should be written out. It is wise to ask only one question at a sitting, and "testing the oracle" should never be attempted. One answer will be sufficient; it is not possible to get a "better answer." The answer one gets is the one answer appropriate to the time and question. If one result is difficult to understand, then a second one may confuse the issue further, or one may actually get the same answer for a second time!

Although they are not runic-inspired, but rather a development of divinatory geomancy, the questions in *Napoléon's Book of Fate* (first published in Dublin around the year 1830) give a good guide to the sort of queries that can be posed to any oracular system. There are 32 questions in this work, which, when appropriately modernized, I have found a useful basis for questioning the runes. They are:

1. *Inform me of all particulars relating to my future wife.*

2. *Will the prisoner be released, or continue captive?*

3. *Shall I live to an old age?*

4. *Shall I have to travel by sea or land, or to reside in foreign climes?*

5. *Shall I be involved in litigation, and, if so, shall I gain or lose my cause?*

6. *Shall I make, or mar, my fortune by gambling?*

7. *Shall I ever be able to retire from business with a fortune?*

8. *Shall I be eminent and meet with preferment in my pursuits?*

9. *Shall I be successful in my present undertaking?*

10. *Shall I ever inherit testamentary property?*
    (i.e., property bequeathed in a will)

11. *Shall I spend this year happier than the last?*

12. *Will my name be immortalized, and will posterity applaud it?*

13. *Will the friend I most reckon upon prove faithful or treacherous?*

14. *Will the stolen property be recovered, and will the thief be detected?*

15. *What is the aspect of the seasons and what political changes are likely to take place?*

16. *Will the stranger soon return from abroad?*

17. *Will my beloved prove true in my absence?*

18. *Will the marriage about to take place be happy and prosperous?*

19. *After my death, will my children be virtuous and happy?*

20. *Shall I ever recover from my present misfortunes?*

21. *Does my dream portend good luck or misfortune?*

22. *Will it be my lot to experience great vicissitudes in this life?*

23. *Will my reputation be at all or much affected by calumny?*

24. *Inform me of all particulars relating to my future husband.*

25. *Shall the patient recover from illness?*

26. *Does the person whom I love, love and regard me?*

27. *Shall my intended journey be prosperous or unlucky?*

28. *Shall I ever find a treasure?*

29. *What trade, or profession ought I to follow?*

30. *Have I any or many enemies?*

31. *Are absent friends in good health, and what is their present employment?*

32. *Shall my wife/I have a son or daughter?*

Using a version of divinatory geomancy, *Napoléon's Book of Fate* gives appropriate one-line answers to these questions. But the answers that the runes give are far more complex than those in any oracular book. Use of the runes enables the runecaster's intuitive and psychic faculties to come into play. There are many techniques for runic divination using stones or cards. Various writers on the subject have had their own favorites, and each method has its own qualities.

It appears that none are better than another at giving an answer to a question, so long as the runecaster is competent. The traditional method using rune stones or wooden slivers (sometimes known as "tines") involves actually "casting" the runes. The rune stones or tines are mixed up randomly by being passed from hand to hand. Then the runecaster, seated on the stol, throws all of the slivers or stones along the right line, in a single cast. The position in which they fall determines the reading. When the runes are cast in this way, some will fall face up, while others will be face down. Only those which fall face up are valid in the divination. In addition, the runes are considered to be "upright" when they face the runecaster and can be read in the normal way. They are "reversed" or "inverted" when they appear upside-down when viewed by the caster.

The manner in which they are picked up varies, depending on personal custom or preference. Some readers use only three runes, while others prefer nine, and some examine all runes which fall the right way up. Some rune readers pick up, in order, the runes that fall nearest to themselves. Others mark a pointer line at some distance from their seat, and the nine nearest to this line are taken. Yet others choose the nine nearest to the right line along the center of the shoat. It is a matter of personal preference and convenience. Choose the method which works best for you. The most important factor in rune reading is the relationship between the runes and the reader. This can be achieved by a series of spiritual exercises or meditations on the runes.

In the Northern Tradition, a runemaster's initiation involves a 24-day long series of meditations, in which each of the runes is meditated upon in the correct sequence. Thus, the meditation for day one will be on the first rune, Feo. For day two it will be on the second rune, Ur; for day three, the third rune, Dorn, and so on, until the 24th day is the day of Dag. It also involves baking 24 biscuits or cakes, upon each of which one of the runes is inscribed or stamped. Breakfast on each of the 24 days consists of eating the corresponding rune biscuit or cake while concentrating upon its meaning. Runic meditation itself is an ancient technique, known in Viking times as *útiseta* or "sitting-out." The "mechanics" of this Northern Tradition meditation involve five distinct factors:

1. *Posture*

2. *Breathing*

3. *Banishment of unwanted thoughts*

4. *Concentration*

5. *The call*

The first stage involves sitting in a definite posture, in a relaxed yet alert position. There are two recommended postures. The first is with the legs crossed, the so-called Celtic posture, as can be seen in ancient images of the gods. The second posture involves sitting with the legs beneath the body, in a sitting/kneeling position.

The second stage is the regulation of breathing: a regular pattern is recommended. This consists of first inhaling deeply and slowly for nine seconds, followed by three seconds holding the breath. Next, the breath is exhaled for nine seconds, with or without the runic call being made, and finally another three seconds of breath-holding. This makes a cycle of 24 seconds for a complete breath.

Third, or concurrently with the regulation of breathing, the visualization of the appropriate rune should be an aid to banishing unwanted thoughts. One may either look at a rune card set up in an appropriate place, or visualize the rune with closed eyes.

The final element is the call or sound corresponding with the rune upon which the individual is concentrating. This technique should be used for a few minutes each day, and whenever a runecast is to be made. After the 24-day initiation period, the relationship between runecaster and rune can be developed and enhanced further by other runic meditations. The best way of meditating runically in conjunction with the information in this book is to use the Haindl Rune Oracle cards.

With the Haindl Rune Oracle cards, the technique of divination is somewhat different from when runestones or wooden slivers are employed. Stones and slivers can be "cast" literally, but cards are not designed to be thrown. Because the use of cards in runic work is not ancient, the techniques followed cannot be those recorded from ancient times. But we are using a living system of divination in a modern way, appropriate to our time, to our experience, and to our needs. "We study tradition," wrote the great French magus Eliphas Lévi, "but we do not consider it to be a critical authority, for it is the common receptacle of antiquity's errors as well as its truths." Cards in general are a relatively recent development in the history of divination. The invention of printing in the 15th century enabled playing cards to be mass-produced from wood block engravings, and, despite ecclesiastical condemnation, their popularity was ensured. K. Frank Jensen's research into the origin of the tarot has revealed that some of the earliest divination books connected with cards came from Germany and Italy in the first half of the 16th century. This form of divination, derived from similar works dealing with divination by dice, depended solely upon individual meanings of cards. According to Jensen, the first reference to cards being used in combination is in the memoirs of Casanova, dated 1765. There, Casanova's Russian lady friend, Zaire, uses the cards to find out what her lover had been up to. As he is returning home one morning after a night out, she throws a bottle at him, telling him that "five rows of five cards each told her everything about the debaucheries that kept him out all night."

Eight years later, Etteilla, the Parisian fortune-teller, claimed to have invented the technique of multi-card spreads for cartomantic divinations. Whoever invented the technique, it is clear that it dates from around the middle of the 18th century. Laying out cards in a spread allows for a much greater flexibility in interpretation. Although many of the spreads were developed for playing cards and tarot cards, they can be used equally well with the rune cards.

The rune cards are shuffled and cut in the usual way of tarot or playing cards. This should involve several turnings, so that there is the possibility of cards turning up inverted. Usually, the reader or runecaster will be doing a reading for another person (who is variously known as the querent, questioner, questor, inquirer, investigator, or subject). It is this person who should cut the pack of cards after shuffling and before they are laid out for interpretation. While doing this, the inquirer should concentrate hard on the matter in question. Then the cards are dealt, one at a time, into the required pattern, or spread. There are a number of different spreads, detailed below. Divinations using more cards are bound to be more detailed, but, as a result, they are more difficult to interpret, and may be more equivocal than those using fewer cards. By experimentation, the reader will discover the method(s) which suit his or her purposes best.

ThE RUNE CARD SPREADS

The spreads given here have a number of different origins. They include patterns derived from the standard spreads used with tarot cards and also the traditional layouts of sacred divination from the Northern Tradition. There are eighteen different basic spreads or methods described here, covering the most simple to the most complex possibilities. In ascending order of complexity, they are: The Single Card (1 card); Pros and Cons (2 cards); The Three Norns (3 cards); The Five Directions (5 cards); The Runic Cross (6 cards); The Vé (7 cards); Tyr's Spread (7 cards); The Runic Wheel (8 cards); The Grid of Nine (9 cards); The Nine-Card Spread (9 cards); The Celtic Cross (10 cards); The Cosmic Axis (11 cards); Astrological Houses (12 cards); The Tree of Life (17 cards); Papus's Spread (19 cards); The "Italian" Spread (22 cards); The Merels (24 cards); and the Circle of Time (25 cards).

Most of these techniques are published here for the first time. Although there are obvious links between the basic and more complex spreads, each of them can be read and used without reference to the others. The names used here for these systems are those that the author uses in his rune work. Where they are the usual stock-in-trade of rune readers, they may go under other names. It is a matter of personal preference. One example is the Five Directions Spread. Michael Howard refers to it as The Cross of Thor, while Ralph Blum has applied it to reincarnation recall, calling it Three Lifetimes. But whatever the name for the more common spreads, the principles are well established by runic practitioners, and will prove useful to the reader.

The Single Card

This is the simplest technique, known here as The Single Card draw, but sometimes called the Odin Card. The deck is shuffled, and the questor draws a single card from it, face down. This is turned over from right to left, ensuring that the orientation of the card (upright or reversed) is maintained. When this technique is used, the reading can be made directly from the listing of rune meanings in Section II, interpreted according to the orientation of the card and the nature of the question.

Pros and Cons

This technique is another simple way of getting a rapid reading. It is conducted in the same way as the previous spread, but instead, two cards are drawn at random from the pack. The combination of the two cards gives the reading. Important combinations of two cards are detailed on pages 236-246. Two cards give a simple, but more complete, reading when their meanings reinforce or counter one another, giving the reader a little more information than would be available with a single card.

The Three Norns

Like the previous two spreads, this is a basic rune card reading which can be conducted and interpreted quite rapidly. Its name comes from the three Norns: Urd, Verdandi, and Skuld, representing the past, the present, and the future. Here, each of the three cards signifies one of these triadic states of being. First, the deck is shuffled and cut, and the top three cards are laid face down on the casting cloth or rug. They are dealt from left to right. Some rune readers lay the cards or stones down in the opposite direction, and read from right to left: however, for more than 3,000 years, the conventional manner of writing all European alphabets has been from left to right.

In the Three Norns spread, the card on the left corresponds with the Norn Urd. It signifies the past actions which underlie the matter in question. The second, middle card corresponds with the Norn Verdandi. It signifies the present: those things and forces which bear directly upon the question. The third, right-hand card corresponds with Skuld, "that which is to become." It represents the outcome of the reading, showing the main trend or direction of the influences which will come to bear if things continue in the same way. Pages 247-250 explain the meanings of the more important combinations of three runes.

There is another, less common, ascription of the runes in this spread. This interpretation does not follow the traditional triad of "past, present, future," but the alternative triad of "first state, action, resultant state." In this interpretation, the first rune represents the present state of affairs, the middle rune signifies the action which may be taken, and the third rune denotes the best possible outcome.

THE FIVE DIRECTIONS

Having two more cards than the previous spread, this reading can provide the subject with additional information. The cards are shuffled as before, and five are dealt, face down. As they are dealt, they are arranged in a cross with a fifth card at the center. Dealing should begin with the first card at the bottom of the cross, the second to the left and above, the third at the top, the fourth to the right, and finally, the fifth to the center. This makes the general movement of the spread create an involuted clockwise spiral. The rune cards should then be turned over, one by one, in the order in which they were dealt.

The card at the bottom of the cross represents the basic influences underlying the question being asked. Rune card number two signifies the problems and hindrances that are affecting the querent. The top rune, number three, represents processes and influences that are acting beneficially on the matter in question, while the fourth rune, to the right, signifies any immediate outcome from the reading. Finally, the fifth, central rune card indicates the influences acting over a longer period than the immediate present. This central rune is the overall influence on the outcome of the reading.

The RUNIC CROSS

This spread uses six cards, laid out with four in the vertical axis, flanked by one on either side. The rune standing alone on the left side signifies the past, while the second card from the bottom in the middle vertical column denotes the present condition of the inquirer. To the right, the third rune indicates the possible future. In the central column, the bottom card defines the basal forces and events that underlie the matter in question—its örlog. The third card from the bottom represents the events which may hinder or obstruct the questor's progress toward the sixth, top card, the likely outcome of the process.

The Vé

This spread of seven cards is named after the traditional V-shaped Norse sacred enclosure, in which worship and divination took place. An important example of such a Vé still exists at Jellinge, the chief royal shrine of Denmark in early medieval times. In the Vé rune card spread, the cards are shuffled in the usual manner and cut by the inquirer. The first seven cards are dealt face down from the top of the pack and laid out in a "V" shape, starting with the top left-hand card, and proceeding in order until the seventh card is at the top right. The cards are then turned over and interpreted, one by one, in the same order.

Each card's place has a specific meaning. The first card, at the top left, indicates past influences. The second denotes the influences operating on the subject at the present time. The third signifies the subject's general future prospects. The fourth card, at the apex of the Vé, known as the key, is perhaps the most important in the reading, for it recommends the best possible course of action for the querent. The fifth card, on the right-hand side of the Vé, indicates the feelings and attitudes of people close to the inquirer, while the sixth card represents hindrances and obstacles which may block the hoped-for resolution to the question. Finally, the seventh card indicates the likely outcome of the matter in question.

TYR'S SPREAD

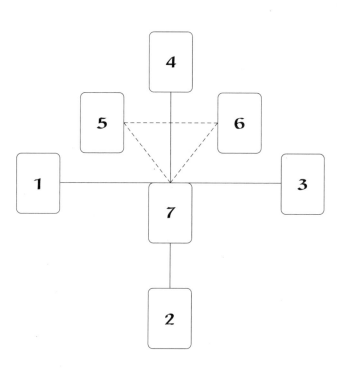

This spread is named after the rune Tyr, whose shape it resembles. Like the Vé spread, Tyr's layout uses seven cards. These are shuffled as before, and cut by the questor. The first four cards from the top of the pack are laid, face down, on the cloth or table in a counter-clockwise fashion, starting with the card lying to the left, in the order: left, lower, right, upper. The spread now makes the form of a cross.

The remaining deck is shuffled again, and a further three cards are dealt. These are placed inside the first cross of four cards in a triangular form. This time, the deal is clockwise, starting again on the left, then on the right, and finally toward the caster. These cards are placed inside the cross, forming a Tyr rune. The first card, on the outer left, represents the origin of the question: the basic feelings and forces which underlie the request. The second card, at the bottom, nearest the reader, signifies the level of highest attainment, the best possible outcome, while the third, on the outside right, denotes the hindrances and obstacles that might block the outcome. The fourth card, at the top of the spread, represents the factors that are likely to cause failure. The fifth is inside on the left, representing the influences from the past, while the sixth, inside on the right signifies present influences. Finally, card seven, inside below, gives an insight into the influences affecting the future outcome of the matter in question.

THE RUNIC WHEEL

In this spread, the basic pattern is derived from the traditional eight-fold division of space. The definition of directions and the measurement of time in the Northern Tradition is based upon an eight-fold division, with the sides of the octagonal figure facing the directions. Each eighth part of the circle is known as an *ætt*. At the middle of each of these eight divisions is the corresponding cardinal or intercardinal direction, which is known as the *ætting*. In Old Norse, the word *ætt* has several related meanings. It can refer to a group of eight things, more specifically a rubric of eight runes or the eight directions of earth and sky. Also, this word can refer to a sector of the sky, a certain direction, and a person's immediate family. Direction, place, and family are connected in the word that defines one's extraction, *ættadr*. This means "belonging by birth or family to a place." Another connected word is ættmadr, denoting a kinsperson.

This eight-fold principle is fundamental in human cultures all over the earth. It is reflected in Native American Medicine Wheels and the Eight-fold Path of the Buddhists. In Tibet, before the Chinese occupation, each of the eight directions was placed under the spiritual guardianship of a specific family, a hereditary tradition of the ættmaodr which is also recorded from Incan Peru and ancient Celtic Britain. This spiritual-geomantic link of a person with a direction-quality of space, once commonplace, is now an alien concept to most of humanity, having been destroyed almost everywhere on this planet by now.

The eight-fold runic wheel has specific runic correspondences which embody certain related qualities. These are the basis of interpreting the divination. To the south is Dag; to the southwest, Dorn; to the west, Kan; and to the northwest, Hagal. The north relates to Jera, the northeast to Eiwaz, east to Bar, and southeast to Lagu. The qualities of these runes correspond with these directions, and so any rune falling in one of these eight "houses" will interact with that quality. The corresponding qualities of the eight runic "house" are thus:

Ætting	Rune	Symbol and Meaning
East	Bar	Great Mother goddess, birch tree, fecundity, birth, beginnings
Southeast	Lagu	water, flow, life-energy
South	Dag	day, the light of high noon, entry, sudden changes
Southwest	Dorn	thorn, giant-power, protection in general
West	Kan	pine torch, illumination
Northwest	Hagal	hail, formative causation
North	Jera	season, completion, fruitfulness
Northeast	Eiwaz	elk's antlers, splayed hand, personal defensive strength

The cards are shuffled and taken from the deck in the usual manner. They are laid out face down in a clockwise fashion in a circle, starting at the east, the spring and morning "house" of Bar. Once all eight cards are down, they are turned over, one by one, again in a clockwise fashion starting at the east. As before, the cards are interpreted according to the inquirer's question and how that relates to the intrinsic meaning of the "houses" into which the cards are placed. The rune of each "house" is examined in turn, starting at the east, and going around clockwise. If a ruling rune falls in its own "house" (a "house rune"), then the meaning of that "house" has great importance to the reading. For example, Bar in the east is a house rune, but Bar in the north is not. If Bar falls in the east, then the qualities of fecundity and beginnings are very important to the inquirer's question.

But if the house rune is reversed, or a rune with an opposite meaning falls in a house (such as a delaying rune like Not), then the quality of that house is negated. Usually, there will be no house rune in the spread. If that is the case, then each rune is considered in relation to the house in which it appears, and a composite answer to the question is built up.

The Runic Wheel and Year-Time Divinations

This universal eight-fold division is the principle which determines the traditional celebrations and markers of the runic year cycle of Central and Northern Europe, and this correspondence is used in divining the appropriate time period for an event or undertaking. Traditionally, there are eight major festivals in this year cycle, based upon the solar phenomena and the harvest cycle. The solar festivals are the two equinoxes and the two solstices. The harvest cycle festivals come between them. Beginning in autumn with a solar commemoration, the eight festivals are the Autumnal Equinox (September 23), Samhain (November 1), Midwinter or Yule (December 21-25), Brigantia or Imbolc (February 1), the Vernal Equinox (March 21), Beltane or May Day (May 1), the Summer Solstice (June 21), and Lughnassadh or Lammas (August 1). In the Christian calendar, three of these "intercardinal" festivals between the solstices and equinoxes are celebrated as feasts: Imbolc is Candlemas; Lammas is the harvest festival; and Samhain is All Saints' Day.

The runes of the directions also represent the corresponding times of the year. South, the "house" of Dag represents the midsummer solstice period; southwest, Dorn, signifies Lammas; the west, Kan, the Autumnal Equinox and the northwest, Hagal, the festival of Samhain. In the north, Jera represents midwinter; in the northeast, Eiwaz corresponds with Imbolc; and the east, Bar, represents the Spring Equinox. Finally, Lagu, in the southeast, corresponds with May Day, Beltane. The appropriate time of year to do something can be determined by using eight cards, one of which represents that activity which the questor wishes to do. They are laid out as before, and the corresponding time period for the "house" in which the card appears determines the outcome.

THE GRID OF NINE

A square grid composed of nine smaller squares is one of the most potent magical symbols of antiquity. Because of its historic use, this spread is most appropriate as a basis for a runic divination. It has several magical connections. It has been used as a protective sigil on artifacts from ancient Greece to eighteenth century Austria. It is the sigil known in Irish magical tradition as The Eight Ifins. Perhaps most importantly in the runic context, this pattern of nine squares in one is the ancient Northern Tradition magical enclosure. The Grid of Nine was used in this context by the ancient Norse shamans in the meditational and divinatory technique of útiseta. Wooden platforms divided into nine squares were erected on top of burial mounds, earth lodges, holy hills, or sacred mountains. The shaman would "sit out" on this gridded structure for a certain period of time, facing north. During this time, the shaman would commune with the gods and gain knowledge.

The Grid of Nine is also "The Magic Square of Saturn." A magic square is a square divided into a number of smaller squares, numbered consecutively. These numbers will be the same as that of any other row. Traditionally, each of the known magic squares is assigned to an astrological planetary ruler. The simplest of these has nine squares, and is ascribed to the planet Saturn. It contains the numbers one to nine, arranged so that each line adds up to 15, and the total of all of the squares adds up to 45. It is the most important magic square of the pagan magicians of Europe.

4	3	8
9	5	1
2	7	6

This numerical sequence defines the way that the cards are placed as they are dealt from the deck. Once they are dealt, they are turned over, one by one, in the sequence in which they will be read. The cards are interpreted as triads. The bottom horizontal line, that nearest to the runecaster, is read first. It represents the past: those factors and processes that have acted upon the subject before now. The card to the left signifies the hidden influences acting in the past; the central card, the basic past influences; and the card to the right, the querent's attitude toward these past events.

The central line is interpreted next. It indicates the forces operative in the present. The left-hand card represents the hidden influences acting now; the central card indicates the present state of events; and the right-hand card signifies the inquirer's attitude toward present events and circumstances.

Lastly, the top line is read. This line stands for the likely outcome of the question. The card to the left represents the hidden influences, hindrances, and obstacles that may prevent the best outcome. The middle card signifies the best possible outcome of the matter in question. The final, ninth card, represents the questor's attitude toward this outcome.

ThE NINE-CARD SPREAD

Briefly, this is a spread derived from tarot reading, and is a variant of the Celtic Cross described next. It differs little from that spread, except in that the second card is absent. In the Celtic Cross, this represents the immediate influences acting upon the querent. The other cards in the spread have the identical meaning as those in the Celtic Cross, and so the reader is referred to that spread for further details.

THE CELTIC CROSS SPREAD

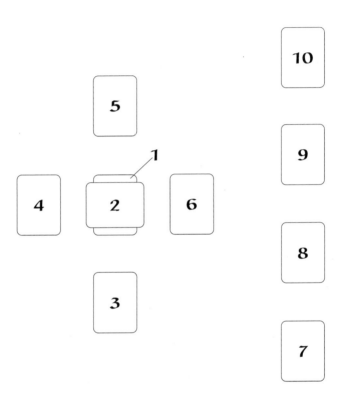

1. *Present position*

2. *Immediate influences*

3. *Goal or destiny*

4. *Distant past or foundation*

5. *Recent past events*

6. *Future influence*

7. *The questioner*

8. *Environmental factors*

9. *Inner emotions*

10. *Final result*

This technique is best known as a tarot spread, but it works equally well with the Haindl Rune Oracle cards. The first part of the spread involves the cross itself. First, the runecaster should select a rune card to represent the inquirer, or subject of the reading. This card, called the significator, can be the rune which corresponds with his or her birthdate. The date correspondences are listed in Appendix III. Alternatively, the rune card can be one which expresses most closely the subject in question. Thus, a question about money would have Feo as its significator, or one about constraints would utilize Not. The significator is laid face up in the reading area. Then the remainder of the deck is shuffled. The first card is turned up, and placed over the significator card, "covering" the symbol of the questor. This represents the general influences acting upon the question, and the general conditions that prevail.

The second card "crosses" the inquirer, and is placed sideways across the first one. It is customary to read this card as upright, no matter which way it falls. It denotes the forces that hinder or oppose the querent.

The third card is laid "beneath" the querent. This indicates the basal influences operating at the foundation of the matter, the querent's own personal experience of the topic in question.

The next rune card is laid to the left of the significator, "behind" the inquirer. This shows the influence which is passing away now, or has just ended.

The fifth rune card "crowns" the significator, being placed immediately above it. This symbolizes any influence which is likely to come into existence in the medium to long term.

The next card is laid to the right of the significator, "before" it, revealing the influence which will be acting upon the questor in the near future.

Now, the layout of the cards is cruciform, and the first part of the spread is completed. But it is not finished yet. The second part of the spread involves the erection of a column of four more cards. The next four cards are turned up, and laid, in order, starting at the bottom and working upwards.

The bottom, or seventh, card (the eighth if the significator is included in the reckoning, which, customarily, it is not) signifies the negative feelings and fears of the inquirer.

The second card of the column, above the previous one, denotes the immediate environment of the querent, which is generally the influences of friends and relatives.

The next card, the ninth, indicates the inquirer's hopes and beliefs.

Finally, at the top of the column, the tenth rune card signifies the final outcome of the matter in question, the result of the influence delineated by the other nine cards.

THE COSMIC AXIS

10   9   11

8

S

6   5   7

4

2   1   3

Consider the Cosmic Axis as a more developed version of the nine-fold grid spread. As with that spread, the bottom tier of three cards represents the past conditions; the middle line, the present state; and the top line, the likely outcome of the question. However, between the three levels are additional linking cards. This is the "cosmic axis" of the spread, linking three worlds together as one. The lower linking card represents the tendencies and influences which have led from the past to the present, and the upper linking card signifies the influences currently leading the condition from its present state toward a future one.

The cards are shuffled in the usual manner, and laid out as follows. The use of a significator, as in the Celtic Cross spread, is optional. If one is used, then it is laid at the central point of the spread, the very center of the shoat. Whether or not a significator is used, the first card of the spread proper is laid at the base of the central column.

This spread can be interpreted in two ways. The most obvious way takes the bottom tier to signify the past. The central card denotes the major influence on the querent in the past, flanked by the subconscious response to the left, and the conscious response to the right. Above this, the linking rune symbolizes the outcome of the influences which have led to the present condition, as indicated by the rune directly above it: the central rune which lies over the significator, when one is used. The left-hand rune card on this, the present level, specifies the subconscious influence acting now, and, correspondingly, the card to the right informs us of the conscious influences. Above the central card, the upper linking card details the result that these present influences will bring if nothing is done to change the situation. Above this, the top tier of the cosmic axis signifies the likely outcome. The central card denotes the major apparent result of the process, with the subconscious effect to its left and the consciously-perceived effect to its right.

An alternative interpretation takes the cosmic axis literally, as it is portrayed in Northern Tradition spirituality. Here, the lower tier represents Annwn, the abyss or underworld, the realm of unformed, unmanifested souls and unevolved matter. The three aspects of this underworld are as before: the unconscious aspect is expressed by the left-hand card, the present actuality or physical manifestation by the central one, and the conscious condition by that on the right. Linking the level of Annwn with that above it is the lower linking rune, which is interpreted in terms of the spiritual evolution from a lower state of existence into the material plane. The central triad of rune cards represents the present, material world, Abred or middle earth. This is the realm in which we exist at the present moment. The three cards are interpreted as for those representing Annwn.

Connecting with higher levels is the upper linking rune of the cosmic axis, which signifies those processes which are tending to accelerate or block our spiritual progress to higher things. Above this is the upper runic triad which denotes the higher plane of existence. This is the upper world, Gwynvyd, the abode of the divine power and those souls that have evolved beyond the earthly plane. The three cards of the upper level are interpreted in the same way as those on the other two levels, except that the central card represents spiritual, rather than material, existence.

This version of the spread can be used to investigate one's spiritual pathway, and one's condition within the shamanistic system represented by the cosmic axis itself. However, because of its sensitive nature, the questor should only undertake this interpretation if he or she is in immediate need of such information. Of course, it should be conducted only with reverence and under appropriate conditions.

THE TREE OF LIFE

S

1

3

2

17

16

4

15

6

5

14

7

13

9

8

12

10

11

Like the Celtic Cross method, the Tree of Life is based on a spread used with tarot cards. The spread's diagram consists of three triangles above a single card, and a line of seven others. In its form, it conforms to both the Tree of Life of the Qabalah, and the Tree of Life of the Northern Tradition.

As with the Celtic Cross spread, a significator card is chosen before spreading the other cards. In the rune card spread, the significator is the card that carries the birth-rune of the inquirer (see Appendix III). This is placed on the table or casting cloth, somewhere toward the presence, away from the operator. After the usual question-statement and shuffling of the remaining 24 cards, the cards are laid out, one by one, from the top of the pack. The shape of the Tree of Life pattern is recreated in three triangles below the significator (toward the operator).

The significator thus forms the top of the tree. Unlike the Celtic Cross spread, where it is covered by the first card dealt, here the significator remains uncovered. The first part of the Tree of Life to be laid out is the upper triangle. This is placed directly below the significator. It begins with the central card, which is followed by the right hand card and finally by that on the left. This upper triangle represents the spiritual world, the ideals and aspirations of the inquirer. Beneath this, a second, middle triangle is laid out in the same way. This one also starts with the card lying on the central axis of the tree, followed by the right, then the left card. This central triangle of rune cards symbolizes the intellectual and moral qualities of the questor. Below this, the lower triangle is laid out in the same manner as the other two. It signifies the inquirer's subconscious desires, impulses, and intuition. Finally, a tenth card is placed below the last triangle. This signifies the foundation of the question in the questor's physical body or home.

The cards are interpreted in the order in which they were laid down. For this purpose, the Tree of Life is visualized as being composed of three vertical columns. According to custom, the cards on the left-hand column of the tree should be interpreted literally, in a formal way. In the Qabalah, this is the Pillar of Judgment. The runes on the central axis may be interpreted in a more intuitive, flexible, pragmatic manner, befitting the Middle Pillar, while those on the right hand side of the tree, the Pillar of Mercy, should be dealt with lovingly and compassionately.

The Qabalistic Tree of Life is an important part of the Jewish esoteric tradition. Like the runes, it is an ancient system which came into being to enable people to classify and gain access to those areas of experience and existence which cannot be fully described in an intellectual way. In the Qabalistic Tree of Life, the ten points or stations on it, known collectively as sephiroth, each have a specific meaning. When enumerated from below to above, the lowest of the sephiroth is called Malkuth, which means "kingdom." This is the basis of the matter, in the earth, the most fundamentally material point from which everything begins its ascent. The second sephirah is immediately above the first. This is Yesod, "foundation." This signifies the emergence of the qualities of individuality from the general earthliness of Malkuth. The next sephirah is Hod, "splendor" or "majesty," which denotes the more apparent results of human actions. The fourth station is Netzach, "endurance" or "victory." This sephirah expresses qualities of endurance and the basic elements of creativity. The fifth sephirah is Tiphereth, "beauty." This signifies the essential self, the middle position between the outward and inner emotions of the individual. It represents the central beauty of that balance in our lives for which we all should strive. The sixth sephirah in this tree is Geburah, "power" or "judgment." In a runecast, this station represents the subject's abilities for good judgment. Next comes Chesed, which means "mercy" or "love," and also represents the inner emotions of the subject in general. The eighth sephirah is Binah, "understanding" or "intelligence," and the ninth is Chokmah, "wisdom." Finally, the top station of the tree is Kether, "crown." In the Qabalah, this signifies the totality of existence, the primordial monad. As "the eye which seeth every precious thing," it parallels precisely the all-seeing single eye of Odin in the Northern Tradition cosmology, a symbol for divine omniscience.

Each of the cards in the spread has a specific significance, based on the qualities ascribed to the corresponding sephirah. The first card at the top of the tree on the central axis (the sephirah Kether) represents the highest intelligence of the querent, while the second, to its right, signifies creative power. This is known as the father card (Chokmah). The third card of the first triangle signifies life and wisdom. This is called the mother card (Binah, the supernal mother, Imma). The fourth card, on the axis below the first, the first card of the middle triangle (Tiphereth), represents the querent's state of balance. This may refer to health, or a willingness to sacrifice something to regain equilibrium in life. To its right is the fifth card, on the station of Chesed, which denotes the questor's good qualities, such as capabilities for love and compassion.

On the opposite side, the sixth card, on the station of Geburah, defines intellectual prowess, physical force, and the power of overcoming opposition. Back on the central axis again, the first card of the lower triangle, the seventh card, equivalent to the sephirah of Yesod, details the imagination, creative physical and mental qualities of the questioner. The eighth, on Netzach, signifies the subject's qualities of endurance. This may refer to lust, sexuality or physical love. The ninth card, on the station of Hod at the left of the lower triangle, represents visible human products. This can refer to procreation; but equally it relates to physical work, the arts and crafts, or any creative products of the individual will. Standing on the station of Malkuth, the tenth and bottom card signifies the querent's home and physical body—his or her "grounding."

In addition to the tree itself, it is customary in this cartomantic divination to erect an additional column, as in the Celtic Cross spread. For this, the next seven cards of the pack are placed face down to the left of the Tree of Life layout. This pack is known as the qualifier or Daath pack. It represents the subject's imminent future, everything in the question which is still in a state of flux, evolution or unfolding. This qualifier is examined only after the other cards are laid out in a straight axial line to the right of the tree, from the bottom to the top as in the Celtic Cross method. They are read in sequence from below to above.

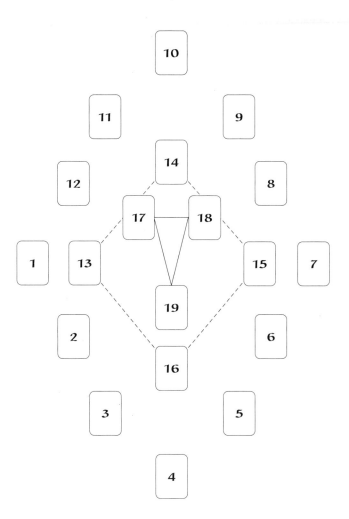

The 19th-century French occultist and Martinist grand master Gerard Encausse, who used the nom-de-plume "Papus," described this spread in his seminal book *The Tarot of the Bohemians* as "the more elaborate process" of cartomancy. It uses nineteen cards, and can be used equally well with runes.

The cards are shuffled as usual, and the questioner cuts them. The top twelve cards are laid out, face downwards, in an "Egyptian Diamond" or Ing rune shape. They are laid out in a counter-clockwise sequence, starting at the left-hand side. Then the remaining cards of the pack are shuffled again, and seven more are laid inside the original diamond. The first of these seven cards is laid inside on the left, while the second card is laid inside at the top. The third of the seven is on the right inside, while the fourth is inside the diamond at the bottom. The final three rune cards are placed as an inner triangle. Card five is placed between cards one and two, while card six is between cards two and three. Finally, inner card number seven is placed directly above card four.

The twelve cards in the outer diamond signify the progression of events signified by the seven inner cards. The first of the inner cards signifies the commencement of the matter in question. The second card indicates the apogee or best possible outcome of the matter, while the third represents any blockages or obstacles which might arise. Finally, the fourth card denotes any possible negative outcome. The final three cards of the spread symbolize the past, present, and likely future of the matter in question.

The "Italian" Spread

This method is based upon what is reputedly the earliest form of tarot spread. It is a version of that said to have been used by Casanova's erstwhile lady friend, Zaire. She used five lines of five cards, while the so-called "Italian Spread" uses three lines of seven, plus one other as a qualifier.

In this spread, the cards are shuffled as usual, and spread on the cloth or table, face down, From this spread, 22 cards are taken one at a time. As they are drawn from the spread, they are laid down in rows of seven. The first seven cards make the first row, then the second seven the next, and the final seven, the last. One final card is drawn which will represent the final outcome or resolution of the matter in question. The remaining three are put aside.

The first column of seven cards denote the immediate past influences on the matter in question. The second column indicates present matters, most importantly to the worries and anxieties of the subject. The seven cards of the final column refer to the immediate future, and the last card is the resolution of the whole matter.

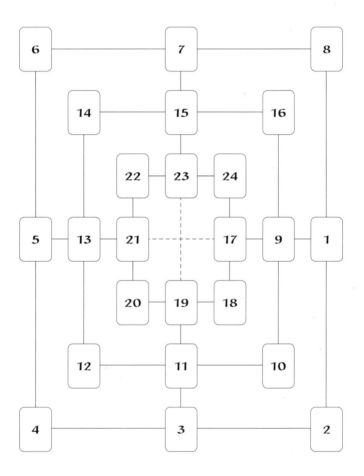

This spread is based upon the ancient pattern or sacred diagram known as the Merels, after the popular game played upon it. This pattern is numbered among the earliest diagrams drawn by human beings, being known from very ancient rock scribings at several far-separated sites. Prehistoric examples of this pattern have been discovered at Hazar Sum in Afghanistan; at Golling and Warschaueck in Austria; and in a cave at Malesherbes, France. An ancient stone game board was excavated from a Bronze Age site at Cr Bri Chualann, County Wicklow, in the Republic of Ireland. Apart from the Irish example, most of these patterns are cut on vertical surfaces, so they could not have been used as game boards. In a similar vein, the device is incised on several ancient tombstones in Britain, most notably at Dryburgh Abbey in Nottinghamshire and at Arbory on the Isle of Man.

Although it appears to have been primarily a magic symbol of protection and enclosure, this design is best known for the board game played upon it. This game is known in England under many local names, but most often it is called Nine Men's Morris. Whatever its name, and there are several alternatives, this game is one of the most ancient still played. Ancient Merels game boards have been found all over Europe and the Near East, including Troy, Kurna (Egypt), Gokstad (Norway), Dublin, Cologne, and London, often accompanied by the eighteen playing pieces.

The square pattern of the Merels board is related to the sacred grid which has been associated with divination since ancient times, representing the diviner's dominion over time and space. The square laid out on the ground was the "mystic plot" in which the officials of the Vehmgericht met. In Viking times, duels known as *Holmganga* were held in similar square enclosures, the forerunners of the modern boxing ring.

The game of Nine Men's Morris need not concern us here, for it is the design of the Merels board itself which is related numerically to the runes of the Elder Futhark. It has 24 points upon which the playing pieces can stand, eight on each of the three squares that compose the "board." Twelve of the pieces are isolated from the other levels, and twelve are in contact with them by way of the lines forming the cross to the center. This pattern is symbolic of the four-square cosmic holy mountain which occurs archetypally in myths from all over the world. It is a plan of the three levels which we have encountered in earlier versions of the Cosmic Axis.

On the Merels board, the central square represents the upper world; the middle square represents the present, the realm of Verdandi and the middle earth in which we live; and the inner square symbolizes the future, the realm of Skuld. Each of the eight points on the three "levels" of the board are taken as equivalent to the eight houses of the runic wheel. On each level, the corresponding direction-qualities of the runic wheel are present. This distribution gives three runes for each direction, one representing each of the triadic states of being; past, present, and future, as well as the corresponding direction-quality. As with the Runic Wheel spread, this diagram has an absolute orientation in space, so it is necessary to be aware of one's directions before conducting the divination. When correctly oriented, the sides of the square should face the four directions, making the connecting-lines between the three concentric squares align with the cardinal directions, the qualities of which are the same as those in the Runic Wheel spread; but here, the runes at the cardinal directions have a greater emphasis.

Ætting	Symbol and Meaning
South	The apex of power accompanied by sudden changes
Southwest	Giant-power, protection
West	Intellectual and spiritual illumination
Northwest	Formative causation
North	Completion at the right time, fruitfulness
Northeast	Defensive strength
East	Fertility, fecundity, physical creation, birth
Southeast	The flow of life-energy

The runecaster can either do a reading in which each of these qualities are examined in relation to the question, or choose one or two of those which are nearest to the core meaning of the question. When all 24 cards are taken into account, a very comprehensive reading is the result.

The Circle of Time

This spread uses all of the 25 cards in the pack. It is based upon a runic wheel of the 24 directions, with a central, axial point, which is the significator. In the runic wheel, each rune is ascribed a direction. Its division is based upon the traditional old European system of dividing things into eighths, a very natural method of apportionment. Traditionally, the eighths are obtained by cutting something in half, then halving the halves to make quarters, and finally halving for a third time, making eighths. In central and northern Europe, further subdivision of the eighths is achieved customarily by cutting each of the eighths into three parts, known in Old English as "ridings" or "thirdings." In the circles of space and time, this triadic division creates 24 sectors. This is the basic geometric division of the day cycle into 24 equal hours.

Each of these sectors has its own corresponding rune of the Elder Futhark. The precise angular divisions of this circle are listed in Appendix I. In some places, this 24-fold division of the circle was laid down in physical form as circles of stones, the European versions of the well-known Native American "medicine wheels." In many ways, especially in their shamanic religion and their reverence for nature, the ancient European and traditional Native American cultures are very close to one another. The most perfect recorded example of these was the megalithic circle known as *Sjöborg,* which stood near Sola in Norway. It consisted of an almost perfect circle composed of 24 large standing stones, regularly spaced. Between, there were 72 smaller stones, also with a regular spacing, making in total an almost perfect 96-fold division of the circle. The 24 larger megaliths marked and symbolized the 24 hours of the day circle. A wooden building in which the councils of eight local districts assembled stood at the center of this remarkable cromlech. Radiating out from this center to the circumference of the stone circle were eight radial rows of small stones.

In this system of divination, the runic row is defined by times and directions, the 24th sector of due south, the direction of high noon and midsummer, is ruled by the final light-rune Dag, and the other runes follow clockwise in sequence. From this, it follows that the southwest ætting lies in the runic sector of Dorn, the west in Kan, the northwest in Hagal, and the north in that of Jera. The northeast sector is ruled by Eiwaz, the east by Bar, and the southeast by the rune Lagu. The directions, and their corresponding runes, are related directly to the appropriate times of day and their corresponding seasons.

The cards are shuffled and laid out in a circle, starting at the east. For guidance, it is best to use a piece of paper upon which the "clock face" of the 24 directions have been drawn. Such a pattern is ideal for embroidering or painting as a "casting cloth." The qualities of the basic eight-fold runic wheel ættir, as detailed above in the Merels spread, are present again in this spread. Each of these eight main runes is flanked on either side by a single rune. Thus, each ætt is composed of three runes: a central main one and two flanking subsidiary runes. Each of these eight groups of three runes is interpreted as an independent triad, as the several other spreads described in this work, including the Merels spread above.

The main rune corresponds to the quality of its direction. The flanking rune to its left, that is, its counter-clockwise side, represents the past influences upon that main rune, and the card to its immediate right, that is, clockwise from it, signifies the outcome of the process. When interpreting the divination, the runecaster can choose to concentrate on a specified quality from the eight directions, or can choose one beforehand by a random draw of a card from the deck (Yr having been removed first). The card drawn will signify the sector of most significance to this divination. This spread can be used also for the determination of directions, when they are required. A single rune can be taken from the deck to divine in which direction something should be located or in which direction one should travel when lost. Thus, if the rune Dag were chosen the direction would be south; Lagu, southeast; Kan, west, and so on. The actual sectors covered by the 24 runes are detailed in the Appendix.

ASTROLOGICAL HOUSES, OR
THE RUNIC WHEEL TECHNIQUE

When the system of "astrological houses" is used for a runic spread, it is called the Runic Wheel. The astrological house system was first developed in Babylon to account for the seemingly erratic courses of the planets. This method of runic divination stems from the astrological connections and associations of these houses.

Technically, the astrological houses are twelve imaginary sectors of the heavens, equally divided, centered on the place where the querent or astrologer is located. In modern astrology, there are various systems of houses, all of which are based upon different methods of dividing the celestial sphere. What they have in common is that in any astrological house system, the first house is placed at the left of the chart just beneath the eastern horizon. The following houses are numbered counter-clockwise, with house number twelve just above the eastern horizon line. Each of the houses refers to a specific aspect of human life and experience, and is ascribed a quality and correspondences that the runecaster refers to when making a reading.

In the Runic Wheel, the runes that fall in each of the twelve houses are considered to represent the following qualities:

1. *The first house refers to the person himself or herself. This includes various personal aspects of the individual: lifestyle, state of health, personality, and general behavior.*

2. *The second house is concerned with money. This can refer to all aspects of personal wealth, property, and financial matters. Gain and loss in the monetary sphere, including theft and fraud, are covered by the second house.*

3. *The third house refers to the individual's relationships with family. This can include letters, writing, publicity, short journeys, and other matters connected with communication.*

4. The fourth house is connected with home life and one's daily environment, fathers and grandfathers, inheritance, especially real estate, including buildings and unsuspected wealth. Most importantly, the fourth house refers to the conclusion of any event.

5. The fifth house is concerned with creative artistic work, recreation, and games of all kinds, including gambling and speculation. It also includes eating and drinking, love affairs, and procreation.

6. The sixth house is connected with the individual's relationship with the world at large. It refers to aunts and uncles, employees, domestic animals, and to which parts of the body are likely to suffer injury or illness.

7. The seventh house refers to the individual's relationship with persons of the opposite sex: sexual adventures, love affairs, partnerships, and wedlock. It also pertains to public enemies, litigation, controversies and conflict in general.

8. The eighth house is associated with death in general and consequent financial matters, such as legacies, wills, and the estate of the deceased. Other aspects of the eighth house are communication with the spirit world and poverty.

9. The ninth house is connected with travel, especially long journeys and relationships with foreigners. This is the house of spiritual matters, science, philosophy, religion, dreams, and divination.

10. The tenth house refers to the individual's career, rank, reputation, fame, or notoriety within a profession. In general, it is connected with one's position in society. The individual's mother is also referred to by this house.

11. The eleventh house is associated with the individual's social relationships, friends and acquaintances, members of philanthropic organizations, and patronage by rich people or organizations.

12. *The twelfth and final house refers to the individual's inner personal life. This includes the person's secret fears, sorrows, and intrigues. It refers also to institutions such as prisons, unperceived dangers, and general misfortune.*

The Runic Wheel technique is as follows: The pack is shuffled, and thirteen rune cards are selected. These are laid out clockwise in the form of a wheel with twelve divisions, with the thirteenth card at the center. For clarity, one may use a board or casting cloth upon which the wheel of astrological houses is drawn or embroidered. It is best if this is oriented properly, so that the houses are in their appropriate directions.

Once the cards are spread, there are various ways of interpreting the wheel. Each of the runes may be interpreted individually in relation to their corresponding "house." Or, if a simpler reading is required, only one card may be examined, which corresponds with the house relating most closely to the matter in question. The central rune is the ruler of the wheel and its meaning must be taken into account when all of the other runes are interpreted.

Clearly, a full Runic Wheel reading will provide a wealth of information, and will take quite a long time to complete. But if Eihwaz falls in the first house, then the runecast should be abandoned as "not fit for judgment." If this unfortunate occurrence takes place, then the runecaster should not attempt a new reading until the following day at the earliest. In itself, such a result indicates that the question is very important to the inquirer. He or she should think seriously before deciding on a second attempt at runecasting.

For guidance, the meanings of the runes with regard to each house are as follows. This table gives the most basic interpretations. For more complete readings, the corresponding runic description in the previous section should be consulted.

The Runic Houses

—∿—

First house *(health, etc.)*

—∿—

Feo upright: good health and happiness.

Feo reversed: health problems, financial loss through illness, and unhappiness.

Ur upright: strength and good health.

Ur reversed: weakness and frequent illnesses.

Dorn upright: caution: take special care of health.

Dorn reversed: stress-linked ailments.

As upright: a long, robust life and a wise old age for querent.

As reversed: aging, with related ailments.

Rit upright: relax, give up bad habits, and alter a harmful lifestyle.

Rit reversed: a visit to an ill person.

Kan upright: vigor, abundant energy, and intelligence.

Kan reversed: a breakdown of health: a nervous breakdown or other mental problems.

Gebo upright: good health and intellectual capacities.

Gebo reversed: a loss suffered through illness.

Wunjo upright: joyous good health.

Wunjo reversed: the loss of loved ones through health or lifestyle problems.

Hagal upright: a healing of one's illnesses, though with difficulty.

Hagal reversed: serious illness, possibly an accident.

Not upright and reversed: exercise restraint to prevent illnesses.

Is upright: frigidity; no change in the querent's health problems.

Is reversed: sterility; no improvement in long-term health problems.

Jera upright: fulfillment and athletic abilities.

Jera reversed: decline, aging.

Eihwaz upright: protection against illness.

Eihwaz reversed: infection, bodily defenses reduced in strength.

Peorth upright: good health according to one's lifestyle.

Peorth reversed: disharmony with surroundings, perhaps leading to sickness, especially occupational illnesses.

Eoh upright: the prevention of illness, keeping fit, sound in body and mind.

Eoh reversed: one is unfit, open to infection and mental instability.

Sig upright: vitality, good health in mind and body.

Sig reversed: the questioner is subject to poor health, especially eye problems.

Tyr upright: vitality, sexual vigor, good health in mind and body.

Tyr reversed: sexual problems in men; for women, sexual problems in their relationships with men.

Bar upright: all aspects of pregnancy, birth, growth.

Bar reversed: take notice of gain and decline.

Ehwaz upright: a personal transformation for the better, improvements, and cures of illnesses.

Ehwaz reversed: sudden illness, and changes brought about by health problems.

Man upright: full vigor in mind and body, strong intellectual qualities.

Man reversed: illnesses may isolate the individual from society.

Lagu upright: a drastic change for the better in one's condition; psychic abilities may become apparent.

Lagu reversed: a change for the worse in one's condition.

Ing upright and reversed: a recovery from illness.

Odal upright: inherited strength, health, and mental agility.

Odal reversed: hereditary or congenital health problems may become apparent.

Dag upright: a sudden advantageous resolution of a health problem; optimistic mental states are required.

Dag reversed: a sudden decline in the subject's vigor, or the onset of illness; pessimism and negative attitudes are probable, but should be avoided.

Yr upright: strength and stability in physical and mental health.

Yr reversed: weakness; physical and mental instability.

—⚒—

Second house *(money and property)*

—⚒—

Feo upright: financial gain, success, and lasting prosperity.

Feo reversed: serious losses, business failures, bankruptcy.

Ur upright: financial strength and security, failure of business rivals.

Ur reversed: possible financial weaknesses, uncertainty, and insecurity.

Dorn upright: safeguarded money and property; security.

Dorn reversed: caution against losses, insecurity, the danger of theft or fraud.

As upright: the wise and prudent use of resources.

As reversed: unwise, rash, ill-considered financial transactions.

Rit upright: financial deals involving travel.

Rit reversed: no movement at present in the situation in question.

Kan upright: the intelligent use of money or property.

Kan reversed: unwise investments; ill-thought-out schemes leading to loss.

Gebo upright: an unexpected gift of money, a tax rebate, or winnings in gambling.

Gebo reversed: loss, outgoing payments, taxation.

Wunjo upright: joyous prosperity.

Wunjo reversed: miserable poverty.

Hagal upright and reversed: the continuation of processes already underway.

Not upright: the necessity to act will lead to an improvement in finances.

Not reversed: beware that one may not act until too late, and be forced into a worse position than is strictly necessary.

Is upright and reversed: no change in the present situation.

Jera upright: prosperity will come in due course.

Jera reversed: decline of prosperity through external agencies, the "business cycle," etc.

Eihwaz upright: the defense of one's property or financial interests.

Eihwaz reversed: poor prospects at present for keeping money or property.

Peorth upright: unexpected gains.

Peorth reversed: past, forgotten debts will have to be repaid now.

Eiwaz upright: monetary problems are defeated by new, positive influences.

Eiwaz reversed: financial and material losses that cannot be regained.

Sig upright: sound financial guidance.

Sig reversed: over-stretching of one's resources will lead to failure.

Tyr upright: long-lasting, powerful material success.

Tyr reversed: short-term gains will presage losses.

Bar upright: the subject's growth in financial terms.

Bar reversed: stagnation of resources.

Ehwaz upright: successful move to another house.

Ehwaz reversed: a warning against restless change from one project to another, frustrating business plans.

Man upright: conflict with others over money or property.

Man reversed: a warning of isolation brought about by unseen rivals.

Lagu upright: a beneficial flow of money and property.

Lagu reversed: financial affairs in a state of confusion.

Ing upright: the successful completion of a project, or the final purchase of property.

Ing reversed: failure to complete a contract.

Odal upright: inheritance of legacies and associated property; consolidation of ownership.

Odal reversed: loss of inherited property, destruction of heritage.

Dag upright and reversed: a sudden change in financial status, from good to bad or vice-versa.

Yr upright: a stable financial situation.

Yr reversed: instability and uncertainty, loss through accident or theft.

Third house *(relationship with family)*

Feo upright: the subject's financial stability will be assisted by family.

Feo reversed: financial losses as a result of family commitments.

Ur upright: personal strength in one's relationship with the family.

Ur reversed: a missed opportunity to help a relative.

Dorn upright: good news from a relative.

Dorn reversed: bad news from a relative.

As upright: good advice from an older relative.

As reversed: problems caused by an elderly relative.

Rit upright: a short journey, perhaps a visit to a relative.

Rit reversed: caution against making an abortive journey; misunderstandings.

Kan upright: ability in communicating with others, especially in writing.

Kan reversed: inability in communicating with others.

Gebo upright: a generous gift from a relative; reconciliation.

Gebo reversed: sadness originating from a close relative; separation.

Wunjo upright: a happy family life.

Wunjo reversed: disruptions of the inquirer's family life: conflict, strife; evanescent happiness.

Hagal upright: the creation of a new public image.

Hagal reversed: disruption of the subject's plans by a relative.

Not upright and reversed: caution is called for when dealing with relatives.

Is upright and reversed: emotional cooling, seemingly irresolvable lack of communication.

Jera upright: the return of and reconciliation with an apparently estranged relative.

Jera reversed: disagreements with relatives, soon regretted.

Eihwaz upright: news of long-lost relatives.

Eihwaz reversed: a recurrence of past hostility, especially concerning difficult relationships with relatives.

Peorth upright: a happy family reunion.

Peorth reversed: family secrets from the past are revealed.

Eiwaz upright: protection of the individual by family.

Eiwaz reversed: warning of the abandonment by relatives; the possibility of being orphaned or disowned.

Sig upright: guidance by helpful relatives.

Sig reversed: questioner may be "led astray" by relatives.

Tyr upright: emotional balance within the family.

Tyr reversed: emotional frustration brought on by family relationships.

Bar upright: marriage, bringing new relations.

Bar reversed: estrangement from one's partner, leading to separation or divorce.

Ehwaz upright: travel.

Ehwaz reversed: the danger of restless inaction; failure of pursuits connected with communication.

Man upright: family relationships; suffering through relationships outside the family.

Man reversed: social relationships outside the family are suffering.

Lagu upright: a journey over or across water.

Lagu reversed: confusion, loss of communicative abilities, especially with regard to one's relatives.

Ing upright and reversed: the completion of a family project; the end of a cycle.

Odal upright: sharing property with one's relations.

Odal reversed: guard against quarrels over property within the family.

Dag upright: sudden changes for the better in family relationships.

Dag reversed: sudden changes for the worse in family relationships.

Yr upright: stable family relationships, but rather rigidly observed.

Yr reversed: disintegration of family relationships in conflict.

—⚶—

Fourth house *(home environment, conclusions)*

—⚶—

Feo upright: the successful conclusion of a deal involving money.

Feo reversed: failure of a project involving money; theft, bankruptcy.

Ur upright: responsibility, especially strong fatherly guidance.

Ur reversed: inconclusive results in one's projects.

Dorn upright: successful precautions taken against theft of one's property.

Dorn reversed: possible failure of precautions against theft.

As upright: accept wise, fatherly advice.

As reversed: reject biased advice from a father figure.

Rit upright: the conclusion of a successful search.

Rit reversed: a warning against a futile search.

Kan upright: the realization of the one's projects; spiritual enlightenment.

Kan reversed: false hopes dashed.

Gebo upright or reversed: a positive partnership in the home environment.

Wunjo upright: pride in one's home.

Wunjo reversed: unhappiness in one's home situation.

Hagal upright: an interruption in the home.

Hagal reversed: caution against disruption, perhaps permanent, of the home.

Not upright and reversed: a long-standing problem concerning possessions or inheritance, the severity of which depends on whether the rune is upright or inverted.

Is upright or reversed: a cool relationship with one's father or a father figure.

Jera upright: the fruition of one's favorite project; a "windfall."

Jera reversed: setbacks; no final conclusions yet.

Eihwaz upright: the transformation of conditions through a death, perhaps indicating inheritance.

Eihwaz reversed: death and the grave.

Peorth upright: imminent revelation of something of worth that has been hidden.

Peorth reversed: a warning of the discovery of concealed loss.

Eiwaz upright: defend possessions—especially buildings—against theft.

Eiwaz reversed: one may be taken advantage of or robbed.

Sig upright: success and achievement in the area of the home.

Sig reversed: retirement.

Tyr upright: the powerful influence of a father or father figure.

Tyr reversed: weakness and lethargy in one's father or father figure.

Bar upright: a protective, nourishing domestic environment.

Bar reversed: domestic problems and disharmony.

Ehwaz upright: a change in the home environment; a move of house.

Ehwaz reversed: caution against a disadvantageous change at home.

Man upright: an improvement in one's domestic situation brought about by applied rational thought.

Man reversed: there may be no improvement in a poor domestic situation, due to one's intransigence.

Lagu upright: the acquisition of possessions through the use of the intuitive faculties.

Lagu reversed: caution against loss of possessions through faulty judgment.

Ing upright and reversed: a valuable inheritance.

Odal upright: successful maintenance of property against threats.

Odal reversed: loss of property, expropriation, confiscation.

Dag upright: the discovery of unexpected, hidden treasure.

Dag reversed: uncertainty over ownership of property; litigation.

Yr upright: stable maintenance of home and property.

Yr reversed: be aware of maintenance problems with property, leading to decline and disintegration.

—⚹—

Fifth house (relationships, love, sexuality, creativity)

—⚹—

Feo upright: success in one's relationships.

Feo reversed: relationships with others will be awkward.

Ur upright: a sudden and dramatic improvement in one's love life.

Ur reversed: a good opportunity should soon present itself, so be aware of it and do not let it slip away.

Dorn upright: take note of a beneficial coincidence, a "lucky break."

Dorn reversed: one may take mistaken actions concerning one's partner.

As upright: use creative powers, especially in the artistic field.

As reversed: one has creative ability, but, at the moment, it exists without the capacity be usefully applied.

Rit upright: a courtship.

Rit reversed: the sudden termination of a love affair.

Kan upright: a courtship.

Kan reversed: a passive partner in a sexual relationship.

Gebo upright and reversed: generosity in love; a betrothal.

Wunjo upright: love, creativity, and contentment.

Wunjo reversed: possible unhappiness in one's relationships.

Hagal upright: further complex relationships, following already-familiar patterns.

Hagal reversed: unorthodox relationships.

Not upright: hostility in relationships; possibly an arranged marriage or marriage of convenience.

Not reversed: a serious incompatibility in a relationship that is kept together for other reasons.

Is upright and reversed: a cooling of relationships, bringing about inactivity and indifference.

Jera upright and reversed: rewarding relationships; feasting and luxury.

Eihwaz upright: the renewal of a relationship which ended long ago.

Eihwaz reversed: the return of old problems in a relationship.

Peorth upright: an unexpected "second chance" in a relationship or love; possibly an affair with a taste for amusement and pleasure.

Peorth reversed: lost pleasures, failures through gambling or speculative ventures.

Eiwaz upright: a warning to avoid potentially harmful relationships.

Eiwaz reversed: keeping bad company; potentially harmful relationships.

Sig upright: relationships will be successful.

Sig reversed: poor personal relationships, leading to mental or other health problems.

Tyr upright: vigorous strength in male sexuality; fathering children.

Tyr reversed: impotence.

Bar upright: vigorous strength in female sexuality; healthy pregnancy and successful childbirth.

Bar reversed: potential female sterility.

Ehwaz upright: the changing relationships brought about by travel.

Ehwaz reversed: uncertainty over changing relationships; sudden changes in one's life; frustration.

Man upright: creative thought; procreation, children.

Man reversed: common human failings in one's relationships may be emphasized; danger from an untrustworthy lover.

Lagu upright: creative artistic work brought into being through the intuitive facility; more generally, conception.

Lagu reversed: a disruption brought about by rapid change, speculation, risk-taking, or gambling.

Ing upright and reversed: a new love affair.

Odal upright: conspicuous consumption, luxury, materialism.

Odal reversed: reduced chances of material success.

Dag upright: sexual relationships will alter rapidly for the better.

Dag reversed: sexual relationships will alter rapidly for the worse.

Yr upright: creativity based on stable foundations will lead to satisfaction and contentment.

Yr reversed: danger of losing a stable base for creativity.

—⚬⚬—

Sixth house (*employees, pets, sickness, injury*)

—⚬⚬—

Feo upright: fair payments for work done.

Feo reversed: problems maintaining the status quo.

Ur upright: one has the physical strength to overcome injury or ailments.

Ur reversed: loss of stamina.

Dorn upright: caution against over-stressing or over-exerting oneself.

Dorn reversed: guard against the possibility of personal injury.

As upright: good management of one's employees or subordinates at work.

As reversed: avoid rumors or bad advice from employees or subordinates at work.

Rit upright: take action at once to avert illness.

Rit reversed: a journey to visit a sick or injured employee or subordinate at work. The possibility of motor accidents.

Kan upright: protection against rumor or bad advice from employees.

Kan reversed: the possibility of burning injuries and illnesses connected with heat.

Gebo upright: the gift of a pet, or something connected with a domestic animal.

Gebo reversed: infections; contagious disease.

Wunjo upright: joy at recovery from an illness.

Wunjo reversed: disappointment at one's failure to recover from an illness.

Hagal upright: notice of sickness or incapacity as the result of a long-standing injury.

Hagal reversed: a long, though not serious, illness.

Not upright and reversed: restraint is called for to maintain good health.

Is upright or reversed: no change in the subject's physical condition.

Jera upright: the period of waiting for healing to take its course.

Jera reversed: the results of earlier actions regarding the subjects of the sixth house.

Eihwaz upright and reversed: illness or death of an aunt, uncle, or pet.

Peorth upright: an unexpected recovery from an injury or illness.

Peorth reversed: the onset of an illness.

Eiwaz upright: resistance against personal harm by human agency, disease, or accident.

Eiwaz reversed: danger from untrustworthy employees or pets.

Sig upright and reversed: a rapid recovery from injury or illness.

Tyr upright: resistance against illness.

Tyr reversed: beware of the threat of sexually transmitted diseases.

Bar upright: a new vigor in the subject.

Bar reversed: decline, reversal, depression.

Ehwaz upright: tackling one's illness in the right frame of mind, bringing healing.

Ehwaz reversed: a visit to a sick aunt or uncle.

Man upright: a new perspective on healing.

Man reversed: a physical injury at the hands of others.

Lagu upright: take heed of premonitions.

Lagu reversed: the possibility of injury through the agency of water; in women, menstrual problems are also indicated.

Ing upright and reversed: the end of a period of one's poor health, heralding a new, better life.

Odal upright: assistance from relatives or long-term employees is on its way.

Odal reversed: a temporary illness through over-work; congenital illnesses; household accidents; disability.

Dag upright: a sudden recovery from a long illness.

Dag reversed: the restraint of one's activities through sickness or injury.

Yr upright: stable conditions at present.

Yr reversed: unstable conditions at present.

—⚶—

Seventh house *(partnerships, relationships, marriage, business, conflict)*

—⚶—

Feo upright: success in financial matters will occur only in collaboration with others.

Feo reversed: collaboration with others may well lead to loss.

Ur upright: good fortune in a partnership or marriage, with the inquirer as the dominant partner.

Ur reversed: weakness, leading to domination by one's partner.

Dorn upright: a mutually-protective relationship.

Dorn reversed: partners in one's relationship may not really care for each other.

As upright: a wise decision will lead to a blessed relationship.

As reversed: an ill-considered decision will lead to an inappropriate relationship.

Rit upright: a choice, one way or the other, needs to be made now between two equally-attractive partners.

Rit reversed: one's intransigence may strain one's relationships.

Kan upright: an enlightened relationship enhanced by knowledge.

Kan reversed: one's relationship may be obscured by lack of openness.

Gebo upright and reversed: love and generosity.

Wunjo upright: a joyful partnership or marriage.

Wunjo reversed: a miserable partnership or marriage.

Hagal upright or reversed: be aware of the interference from a third party or some non-human element in a relationship, bringing problems, the seriousness of which depends on whether Hagal is upright or inverted.

Not upright and reversed: a relationship suffering many constraints; the possibility of litigation.

Is upright and reversed: the achievement and consolidation of a successful relationship.

Jera upright and reversed: the achievement and consolidation of a successful relationship.

Eihwaz upright: the advantageous intervention of "magical" powers in one's relations with others.

Eihwaz reversed: the disadvantageous intervention of "magical" powers in one's relations with others.

Peorth upright: advantageous speculation in business matters, or in a personal relationship.

Peorth reversed: loss through speculation in business matters.

Eiwaz upright: the strength to resist partners who attempt to dominate.

Eiwaz reversed: one's loss of power to resist domination by another.

Sig upright: success in business or conflict.

Sig reversed: success in business or conflict will be counteracted by losses elsewhere.

Tyr upright: perfect sexual compatibility between partners.

Tyr reversed: potential sexual problems in a relationship.

Bar upright: beginnings.

Bar reversed: domestic problems, but with no permanent damage to the relationship.

Ehwaz upright: a new partnership, marriage.

Ehwaz reversed: the end of a relationship, divorce.

Man upright: co-operation with others; satisfying and varied human relationships.

Man reversed: loneliness; lack of companionship or human association.

Lagu upright: go with the flow.

Lagu reversed: one is likely to be misled by his or her partner.

Ing upright and reversed: the completion of a relationship, interpreted as beneficial when upright, and to the questioner's disadvantage when reversed.

Odal upright: the joint property owned by a couple.

Odal reversed: the loss of common property, or the failure of a company.

Dag upright: a rapid increase of profitability.

Dag reversed: a sudden reversal of one's business fortunes.

Yr upright: a stable relationship.

Yr reversed: instability in a relationship, inconstancy, unfaithfulness, adultery.

—ᛘ—

Eighth house *(cessation, deaths, legacies, spirit communications)*
—ᛘ—

Feo upright: financial gain through a death; perhaps a legacy or insurance money.

Feo reversed: financial loss occasioned by a death.

Ur upright: the strength to withstand loss, and to bear the additional responsibility occasioned by it.

Ur reversed: insufficient strength to bear the problems of the moment.

Dorn upright: the cessation of attacks on the individual from whichever direction they may come.

Dorn reversed: one's luck may not be relied on at present.

As upright: spirit communications, especially through the use of the voice.

As reversed: a warning against accepting the testimony of oracles.

Rit upright: funerals, memorial services, wakes.

Rit reversed: a sudden, inconvenient journey associated with a death or closure of a project.

Kan upright: good memories of the dead, biographies, memorials.

Kan reversed: the forgotten dead.

Gebo upright: a legacy from an unexpected source.

Gebo reversed: taxes due to the state upon the death of a relative.

Wunjo upright: joy at the death of a persecutor or tyrant.

Wunjo reversed: sadness at the death of a well-loved friend.

Hagal upright and reversed: the processes of death and cessation acting on the runecast, and their legacy.

Not upright and reversed: poverty.

Is upright and reversed: mourning; inactivity before a
will is proved.

Jera upright: completion; the end of something or someone.

Jera reversed: completion may be impossible before the
cessation of a project or the removal or death of an
individual associated with it.

Eihwaz upright and reversed: a death.

Peorth upright: the influence of unrecognized forces acting
on the eighth house.

Peorth reversed: the unrecognized forces may soon become
manifest, causing change for the worse.

Eiwaz upright: defense against death and destruction.

Eiwaz reversed: defenses may be inadequate.

Sig upright: clear communication with the "spirit world."

Sig reversed: beware of hauntings and demonic interference.

Tyr upright: the will to overcome death and destruction.

Tyr reversed: apparent loss of will to strive to overcome the
forces of death and destruction.

Bar upright: life coming forth from death; reincarnation or rebirth.

Bar reversed: disputes over the death of a relative.

Ehwaz upright: change for the better occasioned by the death
or closure of a project.

Ehwaz reversed: change for the worse occasioned by the death
or closure of a project.

Man upright and reversed: recognize the inevitability of old
age and decline.

Lagu upright: react in a creative manner to the inevitability
of change.

Lagu reversed: change is inevitable, but one is likely to fail to recognize this.

Ing upright and reversed: liberation through change.

Odal upright: a substantial legacy.

Odal reversed: a small legacy, or perhaps inherited debts.

Dag upright and reversed: a sudden inversion of conditions.

Yr upright: monuments to the departed.

Yr reversed: "missing, believed killed."

—ᴍ—

Ninth house *(long journeys, philosophy, religion)*

—ᴍ—

Feo upright: a balanced attitude toward wealth and its use.

Feo reversed: resentment about one's financial position.

Ur upright: belief in oneself and one's abilities.

Ur reversed: a lack of belief in oneself or external realities.

Dorn upright: protection of one's beliefs against other ideas.

Dorn reversed: weakly-formulated beliefs and concepts fall easily to stronger ones, even when the "weak" ones are true and the "strong" ones are false.

As upright: spiritual qualities are emphasized by the querent.

As reversed: spiritual qualities are ignored by the querent.

Rit upright: a long journey; useful religious rituals.

Rit reversed: caution against obsession with ceremony to the detriment of spontaneity.

Kan upright: scientific illumination; a seer's journey toward spiritual enlightenment.

Kan reversed: a warning against obscurity; an inability to see the truth when it is presented quite clearly.

Gebo upright: the gift of insight; seeing things philosophically.

Gebo reversed: failure of the insight, or loss of perspective.

Wunjo upright: spiritual joy; religious ecstasy.

Wunjo reversed: falling into a state of depression, negativity, pessimism, and nihilism.

Hagal upright and reversed: spiritual processes which cannot be hurried.

Not upright: a spiritual reject ion of the material world.

Not reversed: beware of materialism elevated to a creed.

Is upright and reversed: religious inflexibility and intolerance.

Jera upright: patience is required.

Jera reversed: a warning against impatience.

Eiwaz upright: death and rebirth; this may be taken symbolically in spiritual rather than physical terms. Protection on the spiritual level.

Eiwaz reversed: loss of spiritual protection; open to psychic attack.

Peorth upright: the revelation of secret or hidden wisdom.

Peorth reversed: be aware of the unpleasant aspects of visions and revelations.

Sig upright: clarity of spiritual power.

Sig reversed: suppression of spirituality.

Tyr upright: religious self-sacrifice.

Tyr reversed: religious domination by others.

Bar upright: the birth of new faith.

Bar reversed: aborted philosophies, loss of faith.

Ehwaz upright and reversed: a long journey, perhaps emigration.

Man upright: a belief in the essential goodness of human nature.

Man reversed: a belief in the essential evil of human nature.

Lagu upright: the intuitive side of philosophy.

Lagu reversed: misinterpretation of spiritual teachings, misunderstanding of one's place in the scheme of things.

Ing upright and reversed: the individual will be freed from worries.

Odal upright: adherence to the beliefs of one's "roots."

Odal reversed: caution against rejection of tradition.

Dag upright: an optimistic outlook; a change for the better.

Dag reversed: a pessimistic outlook; a turn for the worse.

Yr upright: orthodoxy; religious fundamentalism.

Yr reversed: revolutionary philosophy; iconoclasm.

—∿∿—

Tenth house (career, fame, notoriety)

—∿∿—

Feo upright: an acceptable, well-paid profession.

Feo reversed: hard work for little reward.

Ur upright: hard work brings rewards, such as promotion.

Ur reversed: hard work for little reward.

Dorn upright: protection of professional integrity.

Dorn reversed: professional jealousy.

As upright: receiving good advice: act on it.

As reversed: bad career advice may be given.

Rit upright: careers involving travel.

Rit reversed: setbacks in the subject's career.

Kan upright: publicity and fame in one's chosen field of endeavor.

Kan reversed: obscurity.

Gebo upright: take advantage of a good opportunity.

Gebo reversed: a warning against rejecting opportunities.

Wunjo upright: the questioner's desired accomplishment.

Wunjo reversed: the failure of the accomplishment.

Hagal upright: the causes of success.

Hagal reversed: the causes of failure.

Not upright: avoid seeking notoriety.

Not reversed: caution in one's profession is called for.

Is upright and reversed: no prospect of change in one's circumstances.

Jera upright: things will come to fruition, but only in good time: they cannot be rushed.

Jera reversed: legal problems connected with work.

Eihwaz upright: delays in attaining one's set goals.

Eihwaz reversed: the blockage and binding of one's plans.

Peorth upright: taking risks with one's career is likely to bring success.

Peorth reversed: taking risks with one's career is likely to lead to disaster.

Eiwaz upright: the beginning of a new career.

Eiwaz reversed: beware of potentially harmful outside influences.

Sig upright: positive guidance in one's career.

Sig reversed: a warning not to over-exert oneself in one's work.

Tyr upright: powerful accomplishments, with accompanying public acclaim.

Tyr reversed: accomplishments tarnished by personal problems.

Bar upright: the querent's mother.

Bar reversed: disputes and arguments with authority.

Ehwaz upright: a change of employment; promotion.

Ehwaz reversed: restlessness in employment; the feeling
of frustration.

Man upright: a good reputation, rank, and honor in society.

Man reversed: one's image in the world relies entirely on the self;
there will be no assistance from others.

Lagu upright: go with the flow-the fashionable "signs of the times."

Lagu reversed: it is not possible to follow the "signs of the times."

Ing upright: achievement of a career aim.

Ing reversed: achievement will not be as rewarding as one thought
it would be.

Odal upright: a career in government.

Odal reversed: delay in achieving one's objectives.

Dag upright: a change of one's attitude may lead to fame
and fortune.

Dag reversed: success is impossible without a change of direction
from the present course.

Yr upright: the consolidation of successes.

Yr reversed: a failure to consolidate successes, the problems
of being a "has-been."

—⚶—

Eleventh house *(acquaintances, friends, social relationships, patronage)*

—⚶—

Feo upright: financial gain occasioned by social contacts.

Feo reversed: problems maintaining the status quo.

Ur upright: a progressive change in relationships, from weakness
to strength.

Ur reversed: a weakening of the subject's position in society.

Dorn upright: protection and assistance from someone highly placed; sponsorship and patronage.

Dorn reversed: a warning against too much defensiveness in social relationships.

As upright: benefits to be gained by following good advice.

As reversed: do not reject social contacts and well-meaning assistance in one's life.

Rit upright: now is a good time to enter negotiations with others.

Rit reversed: a warning against intransigence in one's dealings with others.

Kan upright: one will be a prominent figure in social circles, perhaps a former of opinions, or a spiritual leader.

Kan reversed: do not be a slave to convention, or the abject follower of a leader-figure.

Gebo upright and reversed: union, the individual joining with a society or movement; in this case, one with altruistic and philanthropic objectives.

Wunjo upright: a successful and joyful harmonization with others.

Wunjo reversed: the danger of becoming an "outsider," out of touch with others.

Hagal upright: a transformative relationship with a friend.

Hagal reversed: entanglements with bureaucracy.

Not upright: a reminder of the need to work in harmony with society's ways in order to achieve anything positive.

Not reversed: a refusal to do things in the conventional manner, even to the individual's disadvantage.

Is upright and reversed: disagreement with the present state of society, but with a feeling of powerlessness to do anything about it.

Jera upright: mind and body in harmony with the prevailing social environment.

Jera reversed: the need to bring oneself into harmony with the prevailing social environment.

Eihwaz upright: strong, mutually-helpful bonds with friends.

Eihwaz reversed: disintegration of friendships.

Peorth upright: secrets between friends.

Peorth reversed: caution in dealing with friends, especially with regard to joint speculative ventures.

Eiwaz upright: trustworthy friends.

Eiwaz reversed: vulnerability to manipulative social contacts.

Sig upright: strength to one's humanitarian convictions.

Sig reversed: one's worries about social relationships may be obscuring more important considerations.

Tyr upright: a strong motivation to support and further a humanitarian ideal.

Tyr reversed: a warning against using ideals as a weapon—the "holy war" syndrome.

Bar upright: the foundation of a club or society dedicated to the pursuit of an environmental objective.

Bar reversed: an important project is in danger of collapse.

Ehwaz upright: travel in the company of others.

Ehwaz reversed: abortive social visits.

Man upright: excellent social relationships with others.

Man reversed: the likelihood of self-imposed separation and isolation from society.

Lagu upright: flowing and growing social relationships, with a possible teaching role for the querent.

Lagu reversed: one is in an inappropriate social milieu.

Ing upright and reversed: acceptance within a new social role.

Odal upright: any attempts to emulate friends by becoming materialistic will lead to a loss of spirituality.

Odal reversed: attempts to emulate materialists are ultimately futile, and will lead to unhappiness.

Dag upright: a change for the better in social relationships.

Dag reversed: the possibility of a change for the worse in one's social relationships, leading to the loss of acquaintances and friends.

Yr upright: a desire for a stable position in society.

Yr reversed: stability is an illusion.

—ᚲᚲ—

Twelfth house (personal hopes and fears, the hidden side of life and society)

—ᚲᚲ—

Feo upright: successful increase and development of one's secret projects.

Feo reversed: regrets concerning one's financial status.

Ur upright: innate strength and stamina will overcome any unfounded fears.

Ur reversed: one should not act intuitively, driven by hopes or fears, but should wait for more concrete information before acting.

Dorn upright: adequate defense against hidden threats.

Dorn reversed: danger to the questioner in the hidden side of life.

As upright: the eloquent expression, for the first time, of one's hopes.

As reversed: the explicit expression, for the first time, of one's inner fears.

Rit upright: a desire or even a compulsion to keep to "rituals" in one's life.

Rit reversed: a fear of traveling and change in general.

Kan upright: one possesses positive, visionary intellectual abilities, and should use them.

Kan reversed: a danger that one may retreat into fantasies.

Gebo upright: a secret gift, physical or spiritual, from an indeterminate source.

Gebo reversed: giving away one's personal hopes as a sacrifice to help others.

Wunjo reversed: unhappiness, secret paranoia.

Hagal upright and reversed: the forces acting on the subject to form a vision of the world.

Not upright: perceived restrictions on the one's potential for action.

Not reversed: unseen restrictions, possibly legal restraint or imprisonment.

Is upright and reversed: immobilization, imprisonment.

Jera upright: the fulfillment of one's dreams.

Jera reversed: the fulfillment's of one's fears.

Eihwaz upright: the ability to turn the problem in question to one's advantage.

Eihwaz reversed: danger from concealed problems, but one has the power to surpass this danger.

Peorth upright: suspicions of illness, which are probably unfounded.

Peorth reversed: fears of illness may be founded on fact.

Eiwaz upright: membership in an esoteric or magical order.

Eiwaz reversed: one's associates may be deleterious to one's spiritual progress.

Sig upright: a triumphant outcome of the individual's dealings with hostile institutions.

Sig reversed: coming struggles, ultimately successful, against hidden enemies.

Tyr upright: a secret love affair; sexual experimentation.

Tyr reversed: one is liable to suffer sexually-based neuroses.

Bar upright: fears concerning the querent's parents or offspring.

Bar reversed: alienation from one's relatives, leading to life in an institution such as a hostel or prison.

Ehwaz upright: the problem is being dealt with an appropriate manner, and the course of action should be continued with vigor.

Ehwaz reversed: understandable uncertainty with regard to the matter in question.

Man upright: action against hidden enemies or members of secret societies.

Man reversed: regrets concerning the subject's social status, or perceived lack of it.

Lagu upright: trust intuition, and flow with it.

Lagu reversed: intuitive powers are liable to be ineffectual at the crucial moment.

Ing upright: the realization of one's dreams is imminent.

Ing reversed: the destruction of one's dreams is imminent. This may bring disillusionment, leading to cynicism.

Odal upright: one's standing within the family is more important than one's standing in society.

Odal reversed: be aware of a breakdown in communications with others.

Dag upright: changes that have not been considered by the querent.

Dag reversed: sudden change may lead to disaster.

Yr upright: the power to distinguish fantasy from reality.

Yr reversed: misfortune and failure.

SIGNIFICANT RUNIC COMBINATIONS

In a runecast, some possible runic combinations are more significant or forceful than others. These important combinations are used in rune magic as bind-runes. Some runes are more powerfully important than others, and so there are more significant combinations. Unless specified otherwise, the rune with which it is paired is in the upright position.

FEO

With Ur: healing is taking place.
With As: wealth or success through the intellect.
With Sig: wealth through hard work.
With Tyr: power and success.
With Odal: reward through perseverance.
With Dag: increase in wealth.
Upright with Hagal inverted: failure.

UR

With Feo: healing.
With As: the power of sorcery.
With Rit: a change is necessary; the querent has the strength to carry it through successfully.
Inverted with Rit: change is necessary, but strength is lacking.
Inverted with Gebo or inverted Wunjo: the querent is being dominated by a stronger personality than him/herself.
Inverted with Ehwaz and Lagu: an opportunity which should be allowed to pass by.

ÐORN

—ᴟᴟ—

With As, Jera, and Man: attempt nothing on one's own at present.

With Hagal, Is, or Not: it is unwise to proceed with current
projects at present or to attempt anything new until the
time is right.

With Eihwaz and Eiwaz: a condition of protective good luck.

Inverted with Rit: control of the will.

Inverted with inverted Kan: the querent has been outstripped
or surpassed by a colleague or pupil.

AS

—ᴟᴟ—

With Feo: wealth gained through intellectual prowess.

With Ur: the possession of the mystic power of sorcery.

With Wunjo: creative mental effort.

With Gebo: this combination produces the bind-rune Gibu Auia,
which means "good luck," this is the best runic omen for
good luck.

With Jera: take legal advice on the matter in question.

With Peorth: the rediscovery of hidden knowledge.

Inverted with inverted Peorth: forgetfulness and lost knowledge.

With Ehwaz: a journey.

With Bar: a matter concerning the parent/child relationship,
perhaps a visit from a parent.

With Man and Lagu *(in this context these are hog runes)*: wisdom
with Man, and academic prowess with Lagu.

With inverted Bar: concern about a child.

RIT

—ᚱᚱ—

*With **Kan:*** creative work is underway.

*With **Tyr:*** any legal litigation will prove successful for the querent, providing that he or she is in the right.

*With **Ehwaz:*** movement, travel, and change; a journey.

*With inverted **Peorth:*** a promise has been broken.

*With inverted **Eiwaz:*** the querent has been fooled or swindled.

*With inverted **Dorn:*** the querent's will is under full control.

KAN

—ᚱᚱ—

*Upright with **Bar** or **Ing:*** a physical birth.

*With **As, Rad, Wunjo, Hagal,** or **Eiwaz:*** the accomplishment of creative work.

*With **Sig:*** the power of illumination, seeing clearly.

*Inverted with inverted **Dorn:*** one has been overtaken or surpassed by a colleague or pupil.

*With **Not** or **Is:*** delays and a negation of the outgoing nature of the rune.

*Inverted with inverted **Not:*** the querent is attempting to hold on to a futile relationship.

*With inverted **Odal:*** a binding of one's activities.

GEBO

—ᚱᚱ—

*With **As:*** this forms the bind-rune known as *Gibu Auia,* "good luck" so this is a particularly auspicious dyad.

*With **Wunjo:*** the meaning of the combination is "gift of joy." As a bind-rune, this is the sigil used in the Christian tradition as the Chi-Rho monogram of Christ.

*With inverted **Bar:*** concern over one's partner's health.

WUNJO

—ᚹ—

With As: creative mental effort.

With Kan: creative work.

With Gebo: the "gift of joy."

Inverted with binding runes like Is and Not: the prognosis is misery.

ᚺAGAL

—ᚹ—

With Rit: others' ill-wishes will be returned to their point of origin.

With Kan: fertility of mind and body, possibly a physical birth, or the accomplishment of creative work.

With Not: an unexpected event to the querent's detriment.

Inverted Is or inverted Odal: delay is to be expected, or an interruption of one's projects.

With Jera: the querent is attempting to follow an unsuitable career or way of life.

With Peorth: a gain of money by means other than work.

With Tyr: the manifestation of creative, formative abilities.

With Dag: the querent expects failure, and is acting in a fatalistic manner.

Inverted runes: Hagal is a rune of transformation which emphasizes the negative qualities that the reversed runes represent. Similarly, inverted Hagal alongside upright runes has the same signification.

NOT

—⚹—

Generally, Not with another rune represents a binding on that other rune's meaning.

With success-oriented runes such as Feo, As, and Sig: a warning against making previously-planned changes.

With Hagal: a sudden, impersonal, delaying event is liable to happen. But it can also mean that an incoming attack or harmful event is thwarted.

With Jera or Yr: the querent will have to make some kind of recompense for a mistake made in the past. Inverted, Not also indicates binding and delay.

IS

—⚹—

Generally, Is puts a static binding or operational straitjacket upon the meaning of the runes with which it is paired.

With Hagal: delay of one's progress, or interruption of one's projects is indicated.

With Dag: this makes the symbol of the double-axe or Labrys, which is a symbol of inflexible authority.

With inverted Dorn or inverted Not: frustration and delay in the event in question.

JERA

—ɷ—

With As: the querent ought to take legal advice with regard to the matter in question.

With Not: recompense must be made for a mistake one has made in the past.

With Peorth: the possibility of an inheritance.

With inverted Man: a legal wrangle.

With Sig: recovery from illness.

EIHWAZ

—ɷ—

Generally, inverted Eihwaz signifies defeat and failure.

With upright Dorn: protection against harm.

With Sig and Eiwaz: magical protection against all ills.

With Rit: the questor has been tricked by someone else, perhaps leading to severe losses.

Inverted with inverted Yr: the aspects are very bad indeed.

PEORTH

—ɷ—

When the question asked is relevant, Peorth with the upright forms of Ur, Kan, Gebo, Tyr, Bar, or Lagu indicates sexual compatibility. When these, or the Peorth card, are inverted, then problems of compatibility are signified.

With Feo or Hagal: a sudden gain of money, usually unearned, such as a win in gambling.

With Jera and Odal: a financial gain from a legacy or inheritance.

EIWAZ

—∞—

It should be noted that when reversed, Eiwaz is not the same
as the rune Yr upright, and, equally, when reversed, Yr does
not have the same meaning as Eiwaz upright. These are two
separate runes, which, in the Haindl Rune Oracle deck,
cannot be confused.

With upright Dorn: we are protected from all harm.
With Eoh: the same reading, but with a more magical connotation.
With Sig: the querent is shielded from problems.

SIG

—∞—

The power of Sig improves any rune with which it may be paired,
but this may be manifested by acceleration or over-emphasis,
rather than the binding or negativity that we consider bad.

With Rit or Wunjo: the querent is obsessed with work to the
detriment of almost everything else.
With Kan and Tyr: emphasizes the individual's enlightenment and
energy respectively.
With Eiwaz: the shielding power of protection against all harm.
With Gebo, Ing, and Dag: the restoration of balance, and right
conditions for health, including recovery from depression.
With Jera and Man: when referring to illness, the combination
signifies a rapid recovery.
With binding runes such as Hagal, Not, Is, and inverted Dorn:
the effect of these runes is still present, but minimized.
With Eihwaz: the querent is shielded from problems.

TYR

—⁓—

Upright, Tyr in general will tend to reinforce the beneficial, powerful aspects of any rune with which it is paired.

With Feo: power and financial success.

With Rit: this bind-rune signifies success in legal matters, so long as one's case is in the right.

With Wunjo: lasting joy.

With Hagal: creative, formative powers.

With Eihwaz: the magical or personal power known as *megin*.

With Peorth: sexual attraction.

With Sig: power and physical success.

With inverted Man: a fight is indicated, with a successful outcome for the querent.

Inverted with inverted Man: a fight which will be lost.

Upright with Lagu: when the querent is female, a battle for her rights is indicated.

Inverted with Odal: the querent is liable to suffer an accident or accidents.

BAR

—⁓—

With As: matters concerning the parent/child relationship, perhaps a visit from a close relative.

Inverted with upright As: anxiety about a child.

With Man: it is unwise to make decision at the present.

Inverted with Gebo: concern over one's partner's health.

ehwaz

—⚶—

Upright with Rit: a journey.
With Kan: the ego under full control of the will.
With Man: "I am."
With Lagu: confusion and dissolution.
With Ing: longevity.
Inverted with Ur: a change of plans or an unexpected event.
Inverted with Rit or Lagu: a long, one-way journey, perhaps
  a removal or emigration.

man

—⚶—

**Inverted Man with another rune cancels or counteracts
  its influence.**

**Bind-runes of Man with runes such as Odal inverted or Dorn,
  Not, Is, and Bar upright:** the querent should postpone
  any important decision-making until later.
With As: the powerful action of the Hogrunes, bringing knowledge
  and wisdom.
With Lagu: intellectual strength.
With Jera: a legal wrangle.
With upright Tyr: a fight.
With inverted Tyr: a lost fight.

lagu

—⚶—

Upright with As: academic success.
With Tyr: the fight for women's rights.
With upright Ehwaz: confusion and dissolution of the status quo.
With inverted Ehwaz: a long, one-way journey,
  perhaps emigration.

With Man: intellectual strength is being applied to the
  matter at hand.
With inverted Ing: distress and sorrow.
With Dag: confusion.
Inverted with Jera: the querent's minor transgressions
  will be exposed.

ING

—m—

*Upright Ing with another rune emphasizes any completional or
  transitional qualities that it may express.*

With Ehwaz: longevity.
Inverted with Lagu: grief and distress.

OÐAL

—m—

Upright with As or Man: a visionary ideal in the mind, perfect
  expression of the will in action.
With Feo, Jera, or Bar: miserliness and materialism.
With Ur and Peorth: the querent will succeed through
  persistence.
With Dag: increase in prestige.
With inverted Tyr: the querent is likely to suffer an accident.
Inverted with Hagal: delay and interruption.
With Man: delay any imminent decision-making.
With Dag: pessimistic thinking is predominant at the present time.

ÐAG

—⟋ɰ⟍—

Bad inverted runes are altered to little more than delayers
by being paired with Dag.

With Feo: an increase in wealth.

With Bar and Lagu: the growing expansive qualities of these runes
are enhanced.

With Dorn: intransigence.

With Not or Is: negative, binding qualities of these runes
are minimized.

With Is: the figure of the Labrys so created may signify inflexible,
authoritarian behavior.

With Lagu: confusion.

With Odal: an increase in prestige.

With Wunjo or Man inverted: the querent is thinking negatively.

ᚣR

—⟋ɰ⟍—

It should be noted that reversed Yr does not have the same
meaning as Eiwaz upright, and, equally, reversed Eiwaz
is not the same as Yr upright.

With Gebo: a happy marriage or partnership, a compensation
for unselfishness.

With Dag: a change from a seemingly good position to a bad one.

Powerful combinations of three runes will occur in the Three Norns, Grid of Nine, Cosmic Axis, Merels, and Circle of Time spreads. Unlike the combinations previously described, these runes should appear in the correct order, read from left to right, as some of them make key words in runic tradition. Sometimes, but not often, this meaning overrides the exoteric meaning of the three runes together. Usually, the runic kennings and the meaning of the word are in perfect alignment with one another. Unless noted otherwise, the runes appear in their upright mode.

Ur, Lagu, and *Feo* combine to make the magical word ULF, signifying the almost irresistible power of the wolf. In a divination, this signifies a powerful force assisting the inquirer.

Dorn reversed, Is, and *Not* together represent an irresistible force of binding and delay acting upon the inquirer. The only thing to do in such circumstances is to abandon the project of circumstance in question, and change course.

As, Lagu, and *Ur* make the magical word ALU, which signifies the "water of life"—ale—literally the water of the primal power of the gods. It is a strong combination which promises good things, changes for the better. The word *alu* signifies ecstasy and divine guardianship, being connected with *loegr,* magic power. In a divination, these qualities are working for the questor's benefit.

The triad of *As, Feo,* and *Ing* represent release from a problematic situation, indicating that those things tangling up or binding one's life will soon be broken through or passed by.

Together, *As, Wunjo,* and *Odal* signify the triadic aspects of the Allfather, manifested as the deities Odin, Vili, and Vé. In a runecast, this triad indicates that perfect harmony of one's life with one's will can be achieved if one continues on the chosen path.

As, Sig, and **Kan** combine to make the runic word ASC, Yggdrassil, the sacred ash tree of the gods. This represents the power to survive attacks and to come through adversity unscathed.

Kan, Dag, and **Sig** denote brilliant illumination of the unconscious, the brightness of high day in the physical world, and the light of the sun illuminating the conscious. It is a runic triad of enlightenment, denoting a new approach to problem-solving.

Gebo, As, and **Rit** combine to make the word GAR, the name of the spear of Odin. A beneficial power will soon be brought to the questor's assistance.

The triad of *Gebo, Ing,* and **Ehwaz** tell the inquirer that the matter in question will have a long duration.

Gebo, Man, and **Wunjo** signify reconciliation, the healing of wrongs and hurts between people, and a more harmonious future.

Gebo, Yr, and **Wunjo** together represent the attainment of stable, unselfish contentment.

Wunjo, Odal, and **Dag** combine to make the word WOD, the element in the Anglo-Saxon name Woden (a version of the name Odin), which has the meaning of divine shamanic inspiration. As a rune reading, it indicates the joyful transformation of a seemingly-bad situation through inspired action.

Generally, triadic combinations of the early winter runes *Hagal, Not,* and *Is* denote delay and binding. The combination *Hagal, Is,* and *Not,* making the word HIN, denotes a distancing and a hindering of things from their due course. In a reading, this combination signifies a massive binding and delay acting upon the querent, severely restricting her or his actions.

Similarly, *Not, Is,* and *Lagu* is a triad of negation, the English word "nil" (null), which denotes nothingness. This triad presages the total destruction or obliteration of the matter in question if measures are not taken immediately to avert the disaster.

Jera, Feo, and **Wunjo** represent unification, leading to an abundant, joyful life.

Jera, Ur, and *Sig* signify that the process of healing of the illness, or solution of the problem, is taking place.

Jera, Rit, and *Dorn* combine to make the runic power-word Jro* (Jörth), "the earth." In a reading, this signifies the return of appropriate conditions, but only if the querent is willing to work in harmony with "the way of the world."

Eiwaz, Odal, and *Dorn* signify powerful protection. Interpreted in a reading, they inform us that we are correct in taking the action in question, and that we are defended against any bad consequences which might result.

Peorth, As, and *Rit* indicate that hidden or forgotten knowledge will be recovered. In a reading, this means that the inquirer should make further investigations, as some important factor has likely been overlooked.

Peorth, As, and *Not* signify that one must come into harmony with the necessary processes of existence, or the will of the gods. These three runes make the name of the Great God PAN.

Sig, Odal, and *Lagu* combine to make the name of the solar goddess SÓL, indicating the brilliant energy of the sun. In a reading, this combination indicates that the inquirer has the strength and stability to cope well with any change which may be imminent.

Sig, Tyr, and *Rit* indicate that the querent will be very successful in any upcoming conflicts, especially justified legal actions.

The alignment of the runes *Tyr, Yr,* and *Rit* creates the word TYR, the name of the Northern divinity of strength and success. But Tyr's success is through self-sacrifice for the greater good, and in a runecast it indicates that obstacles will be overcome through individual effort, but that the greater good, rather than the individual, will be served.

Similarly, *Bar, As,* and *Rit* combine to make the word BAR, whose runic meaning is the bear, or, more precisely, the power of a show of strength as the best means of defense. In a reading, this can mean that one may be able to bluff one's way through a confrontation without having to use force, either physical or legal. It tells the questor to stand firm and resist all pressures.

Ehwaz, As, and *Man* denote that the application of one's knowledge to the question will bring a fortunate result that shows wise judgment.

Ehwaz, Ing, and *As* signify that there will be a closer union between the querent and the more mystic secrets of life.

Ing, Not, and *Gebo* make the word ING, which signifies generative power. It is composed of the rune Ing itself, necessity and the gift of the gods.

Odal, Not, and *Dag* combine to make the runic word ÖND, the vital breath or universal soul of all things. It signifies the overcoming of seemingly insuperable problems by aligning oneself with the necessity of the circumstances, and by so doing, transcending them. *Odal, Yr,* and *Wunjo* signify a contented, settled life.

Dag, Rit inverted, and *Lagu,* or *Dag, Ehwaz,* and *Lagu* herald confusion and disruption to one's projects. When these triads appear, then it is time to delay decisions and re-appraise the situation.

Odal, Dorn, and *Rit* make the name of ODR (Othr), one of the consorts of the goddess Freyja. In a reading it signifies the balance between stability and motion, the wish to explore other areas outside those which are accepted as "normal" or "conventional."

CONCLUSION:
THE ATTAINMENT OF WUNJO

Nowadays, as ever, it is possible to have a direct experience of the divine. It can come spontaneously, or more probably through the techniques of shamanry, útiseta, and divination. This is possible because there is no definite boundary between the self and the non-self, between the individual and the "rest of" existence, including that which we term "the divine."

Many spiritual traditions, including that from which the runic system originates, teach that elements of consciousness and spirit are diffused throughout the universe. Nature is neither a dumb brute nor a machine. It is a physical manifestation of the divine spirit, which should be worked with and lived in, not dominated, mistreated, and exploited. The ancient followers of the divine prophet Orpheus saw it personified in the Great God Pan:

—⁓—

I call strong Pan, the substance of the whole,

Ethereal, marine, earthly, general soul,

Undying fire; for all the world is thine,

And all are parts of thee, O pow'r divine…

All parts of matter, various form'd, obey,

All Nature's change thro' thy protecting care,

And all mankind thy lib'ral bounties share,

For these where'er dispersed thro' boundless space,

Still find thy providence support their race.

The Orphic Hymn to Pan, Translated by Thomas Taylor, 1878

It is a fact of existence, recognized by everyone, that we cannot make a flag fly against the wind, or a piece of wood float upstream. On a more general scale, anything which is against nature cannot endure indefinitely. It must come to an end relatively soon, and then nature's balance must be restored once more. Similarly, as individuals, we must follow the laws of nature: the present impending ecological catastrophe is a result of several generations of humanity ignoring this salient fact of life. But disaster is not inevitable, for with conscious realization, human beings can turn away from destructive ways and start living with and for instead of apart from and against nature.

Despite centuries of abuse and neglect, nature is by no means spiritually dead. Whether or not it is recognized by human beings, spirituality is inherent in nature. It is manifest there for any of us who care to look. Runic is a manifestation of this spirituality inherent in nature. It is a system of genuine value, rooted in the collective psyche of human beings, who are part of nature. These eternal truths of existence have been present in human cultures throughout time. When they have been consciously part of the fabric of those cultures, they have enriched people's lives. Human societies, ancient and modern, have been based on the same human reality. We are separated from our ancestors only by the barriers of time, both physical and spiritual. The ancient myths still express eternal truths, but truths whose message has been distorted, marginalized, and even suppressed by the material and organizational demands of industrial society.

Clearly, our age is in need of a retronuevo expression of these fine perceptions which were accepted as normal—indeed, essential—by ancient society. Consciousness-expanding techniques and systems such as the runes are a re-statement of these ancient, eternal forms in a manner appropriate to the present day, without being compromised by the life-denying elements of modern existence. The Haindl Rune Oracle cards are a unique pictorial means of access to the inner spiritual meaning of these archetypal symbols. Through them, ancient skills and wisdom can be reintegrated into modern awareness, thereby extending the blinkered horizons far beyond the preoccupations of materialism.

Studying and using the runes can help us to recognize the dynamic polarities which are at the basis of our lives. The runes can assist the regeneration of those spiritual roots which we all possess, expanding our freedom. Hermann Haindl's rune card for Wunjo shows this access to the apex of joy through a braided, interlaced, entwined, bound, and knotted "tangled thread"—the pathway of life. On our conscious side, the rose of love and pain expresses the law of the unity of opposites, and on the unconscious, the direct, straight, ritual pathway which we can take to our spiritual objective in life. In this way, Wunjo is the harbinger of the transcendent spirit in humanity.

Through the runes (and other elements of ancient wisdom from the world over), we can discover consciously the hidden possibilities of communication beyond the level of the material and the exclusively human. A proper, appropriate use of the runes can help us to deal creatively with the conditions in which we find ourselves living today. In the words of the playwright Eugene O'Neill, this is the essence of "the creative pagan acceptance of life."

Ka!

APPENDIX I
THE BASIC MEANINGS
OF THE RUNES

Feo	Cattle, wealth
Ur	Aurochs, primal strength
Dorn	Thorn, giant-power, protection
As	God-power, speech, intellectual power
Rit	Riding, wheel, motion, ritual process
Kan	Pine torch, light in the darkness, spiritual illumination
Gebo	Gift of the gods, talent/burden
Wunjo	Joy, contentment, prosperity
Hagal	Hall, formative causation
Not	Need, necessity, binding
Is	Ice, cessation, static power
Jera	Season, completion, fruitfulness, return
Eihwaz	Yew tree, bow and arrow, physical and magical defense, mystery of life and death
Peorth	Dice cup, womb, dance of life
Eiwaz	Elk, swan, splayed hand, defensive strength, resistance
Sig	Sun, brightness, energy, success
Tyr	The god Tyr, sword, power, male sexuality
Bar	Great Mother Goddess, birch tree, fecundity, birth, female sexuality

Ehwaz	Horse, motion, transformation, partnership
Man	Human being, mediator between heavens and earth
Lagu	Water, flow, life-energy, subconscious mind
Ing	The god Ing, fire, fertility, limitless expansion and protection
Odal	Homestead, enclosure, ancestral property, possession
Dag	Day, the light of high noon, entry, sudden changes
Yr	The cosmic axis, Yggdrassil or Irminsul, centrality, stability

APPENDIX II
THE RUNIC "HOUSES"
OR SECTORS

The 24 runic "houses" or sectors are defined geometrically. Each "house" occupies a 15° portion ($^1/_{24}$) of the whole circle. Each of the ættings defines the central point of a sector, which means that the 24-rune circle commences at one forty-eighth part of a circle westward of due south (7° 30' west of south). When laid out in terms of the clock face, the runes correspond with the following hours:

Feo	12.30 - 13.30
Ur	13.30 - 14.30
Dorn	14.30 - 15.30
As	15.30 - 16.30
Rit	16.30 - 17.30
Kan	17.30 - 18.30
Gebo	18.30 - 19.30
Wunjo	19.30 - 20.30
Hagal	20.30 - 21.30
Not	21.30 - 22.30
Is	22.30 - 23.30
Jera	23.30 - 00.30
Eihwaz	00.30 - 01.30
Peorth	01.30 - 02.30
Eiwaz	02.30 - 03.30
Sig	03.30 - 04.30

Tyr	04.30 - 05.30
Bar	05.30 - 06.30
Ehwaz	06.30 - 07.30
Man	07.30 - 08.30
Lagu	08.30 - 09.30
Ing	09.30 - 10.30
Odal	10.30 - 11.30
Dag	11.30 - 12.30

The rune Yr is not part of the day and year circle. When it is used, it signifies the unchanging central point around which the year rotates.

APPENDIX III
RUNIC TIME-
CORRESPONDENCES

These are the calendar dates on which each rune in the time cycle of the year commences. These dates can be used for determining the significator card in Celtic Cross, Tree of Life, and Circle of Time rune card readings. Times given are in Local Apparent Time, that is, by the sun, and not according to local commercial time zones. Times are "rounded off" to the nearest whole hour.

Feo	3.00 June 29 until 8.00 July 14
Ur	8.00 July 14 until 14.00 July 29
Dorn	14.00 July 29 until 19.00 August 13
As	19.00 August 13 until 0.00 August 29
Rit	0.00 August 29 until 6.00 September 13
Kan	6.00 September 13 until 11.00 September 28
Gebo	11.00 September 28 until 16.00 October 13
Wunjo	16.00 October 13 until 22.00 October 28
Hagal	22.00 October 28 until 3.00 November 13
Not	3.00 November 13 until 8.00 November 28
Is	8.00 November 28 until 14.00 December 13
Jera	14.00 December 13 until 19.00 December 28
Eihwaz	19.00 December 28 until 1.00 January 13
Peorth	1.00 January 13 until 5.00 January 28
Eiwaz	5.00 January 28 until 10.00 February 12

Sig	10.00 February 12 until 16.00 February 27
Tyr	16.00 February 27 until 21.00 March 14
Bar	21.00 March 14 until 12.00 March 30
Ehwaz	2.00 March 30 until 7.00 April 14
Man	7.00 April 14 until 12.00 April 29
Lagu	12.00 April 29 until 18.00 May 14
Ing	18.00 May 14 until 23.00 May 29
Odal	23.00 May 29 until 4.00 June 14
Dag	4.00 June 14 until 3.00 June 29
Yr	Like Wyrd, ever present, but not used as a significator

APPENDIX IV
GENERAL CORRESPONDENCE
OF THE RUNES

These are the correspondences of each rune with its appropriate tree, polarity, element, and Northern Tradition deity, as used throughout this work. They are not the only possible correspondences; but these are accepted by many American and English rune practitioners, and the author has found them useful in his own rune work. When doing runic meditations, the reader will find these correspondences fruitful.

RUNE	TREE	POLARITY	ELEMENT	GODDESS/GOD
Feo	elder	female	fire/earth	Frey/Freyja/ Fulla/Lofn/ Boann
Ur	birch	male	earth	Thor/Urd/ Eir/Airmed
Dorn	oak/ thorn	male	fire	Thor
As	ash	male	air	Odin, the Æsir in general
Rit	oak	male	air	Ing/Nerthus
Ken	pine	female	fire	Heimdall/ Freyja/Frey/ Nerthus
Gebo	ash/ elm	male/ female	air	Odin/ Friagabis/ Freyja/Gefn

RUNE	TREE	POLARITY	ELEMENT	GODDESS/GOD
Wunjo	ash	male	earth	Odin/Vintios
Hagal	yew	female	ice	Urd/Hela/ Mordgud/ Heimdall
Not	beech/ rowan	female	fire	Nott/Skuld/Var
Is	alder	female	ice	Rinda/Verdandi
Jera	oak	male/female	earth	Frey/Freyja
Eihwaz	yew	male	all	Ullr/Vuldr/ Holler
Peorth	beech/ aspen	female	water	Frigg/Lady Luck
Eiwaz	yew/ service	male/ female	air	Heimdall/ Cernunnos
Sig	juniper/ bay	male	air	Balder/Thor/ Sól/Sunna/ Barbet
Ehwaz	oak/ash	female/ male	earth	Frey/Freyja/ Odin
Man	holly	female/ male	air	Rig-Heimdall/ Odin/Frigg
Lagu	willow	female	water	Njord/Nerthus
Ing	apple	male/ female	water/ earth	Ing/Yngvé-Frey
Odal	hawthorn	male	earth	Odin
Dag	spruce	male	fire/air	Heimdall/Balder
Yr	yew	female/ male	fire/air/ice earth/water	Odin/Frigg/ Vidar

Appendix V
Glossary of Names and Terms Used in This Work

These technical terms come from the Northern Tradition. They are specific words which have specific meanings for which there may be no parallels in modern European languages. The origin of each word is noted.

Abred	The material world = Midgard (W), see *Midgard*
Ætheling	Member of the Anglo-Saxon noble class
Ætt	Eighth of the horizon, one of the eight compass directions (N), see *Airt*
Airmed	Goddess of medicine and healing (I)
Airt	Point of the compass, direction of the wind, a way (S)
Alraune	Image in human form made from the root of bryony or ash (G)
Annwn	The underworld (W)
Asgard	The abode of the gods (N)
Balder	Norse solar god
Berchta	Goddess of growing things, and guardian of as-yet-unborn souls (G)
Beltane	The May Day festival (April 30 eve/May 1) (I, OE, S)
Boan	The cow-goddess (I)
Bragi	God of poetry and eloquence (N)
Brigantia	Pagan festival of January 31 eve/February 1 = Imbolc, Oimelc (I), Candlemas (OE), Lichtmesse (G)

Byrnie	Coat of chain mail (N)
Calas	Solidity, one of the three states of being in Bardic cosmology (W)
Eir	Goddess of Medicine (N)
Externsteine	Outcrop of rocks near Horn in the Teutoburger Walk; The Teutonic sacred place of power (G)
Frey(r)	"The Lord"; God of fertility and creativity (N)
Frigabis	The "free giver" goddess (N)
Galderdikt	Calling runic sounds, incantations
Gefn	"The Giver" goddess (N)
Gutatros	A Celtic shaman, literally an invoker (Ga)
Gwynvyd	The upper world, literally "the White Land" = the Norse Asgard (W)
Harigast	Ancient Teutonic war-deity
Heimdall	The watcher-god (N)
Hela	The goddess of death and the underworld (N)
Heriot	Gift, often a sword, given to a warrior by a war-lord or king
Holmganga	Single combat, literally "going on an island" (N)
Ing	God of protection and fertility (= Frey, q.v.) (OE)
Irminsul	The sacred Teutonic world-pillar, representing the world-tree, the parallel of Yggdrassil, set up at what is now the town of Ober-Marsberg, Germany (G)
Jörmungand	The world serpent = Midgardsorm (N)
Kenning	Poetic allusion or metaphor (OE)
Lofn	Goddess of forbidden love (N)
Mattr	Personal magical power, see *Megin*
Megin	A personal force, distinct from strength or physical power, the possession of which assures good fortune (N)

Merels	A board game, played on a cosmically-symbolic board, whose object is to make a mill, or line of three playing pieces (F)
Mordgud	Goddess who guards the entrance to the underworld (N)
Njörd	God of seafaring, stiller of fire and the waves (N)
Norns	The three parts of existence, personified as Skuld, Urd, and Verdandi. (N) = the Weird Sisters (OE), see *Skuld, Urd, Verdandi*
Nwyvre	The universal life-breath or force = önd, prana, ki (w) (cf. Voivre)
Odin	God of inspiration, poetry, and combat (N)
Ódhr	Inspiration (N)
Önd	The universal life breath or force = Nwyvre (N)
Örlog	literally "primal layers" or "primal laws" that which makes "now" (N)
Ragnarök	Cataclysmic destruction of the world, followed by a regenerated new age ruled by the god Vidar (N), see *Vidar*
Retroneuvo	Basic traditional elements used and interpreted in a new way, appropriate to the present day (A)
Rinda	Goddess of the frozen earth (N)
Rig (r)	By-name of Heimdall, legendary organizer of human society (N), see *Heimdall*
Rune	Character from the ancient Germanic alphabet
Run rig	Traditional Scottish land-allocation using runes (S)
Runic Hour	Hour in the day corresponding to a specific rune
Samhain	Pagan festival of death/rebirth, Eve of October 31/November 1 (C) = Halloween (E)
Shoat	The area over and along which runestones or slivers are thrown in rune-casting (A-S, E)
Skuld	The third Norn, That which is to become = the future (N)

Sliver	A flat slice of wood cut to bear runes for divination or as a talisman (EA)
Tyr	God of self-defense, "The Valiant" (N)
Urd(a)	The First Norn, That which was = the past
Var	Goddess who punish oath-breakers (N)
Verdandi	The second Norn, That which is becoming = the present (N)
Vidar	Son of Odin, god of the New Age after Ragnarök (N), see *Odin*
Vintios	The wind-god (Ga)
Völva	A wise woman (N)
Walpurgisnacht	Walpurgis' Night, May Eve (April 30, the festival of Beltane (G)
Wortcunning	Skill in the knowledge and use of herbs (OE)
Wyrd	One's personal "fate" or "destiny," but also generally "the way things go" (A-S)
Yarthkin	Earth spirit, troublesome or harmful to humans (EA)
Yngvé-Frey	By-name of Ing (N), see *Ing*
Yggdrassil	Literally "the horse of Ygg" (A by-name of Odin); the cosmic axial world tree of Norse tradition (N), see *Odin*
Yule	The festival of midwinter, now amalgamated with Christmas (E, EA, N, Sc)
Zisa	Goddess-consort of Tyr, see *Tyr*

Abbreviations

A	American
E	English
EA	East Anglian
F	French

continued...

G	German
Ga	Gaulish
I	Irish
N	Norse
OE	Old English
S	Scots
W	Welsh

NOTES

NOTES